Praise for *The Trouble With Fairy Tales*

"Reading *The Trouble with Fairy Tales* is like a delightful conversation with a witty, wise, wry friend who splits open those myths we grow up with, the ones that both sustain us and entrap us. Plum Johnson has done it again."

—**Jeannette Walls, #1 bestselling author of**
The Glass Castle* and *Hang the Moon

"Prince Charming, Bluebeard, the Pied Piper and more—Plum Johnson brings to vivid, infuriating, seductive life the whole repertoire of mythic men around whom women were expected to centre their lives. Turning every stereotype inside out and upside down, she is funny, thought-provoking and devastatingly honest. It's not that she can't be thrown off course by what she calls 'the lure of lust' and 'the unalterable inheritance of biology,' but she picks herself up and sets off on a new adventure. A tonic for readers of every age."

—**Katherine Ashenburg, award-winning author of**
Margaret's New Look* and *The Mourner's Dance

"This memoir of love reminds us that fairy tales course with darkness. Plum Johnson describes with great clarity of prose and heart how the men she's loved didn't exist except in her own longing. And we long with her. . . . You'll find yourself in this brave and thoughtful book, if you dare to look into the mirror."

—**Cathrin Bradbury, author of**
This Way Up* and *The Bright Side

"A fascinating cautionary tale told with verve and wit, *The Trouble with Fairy Tales* explores the complexity of our individual realities and the hollowness at the heart of the very things we are taught to value and desire."

—**Mary Lawson, internationally bestselling author of**
Crow Lake* and *A Town Called Solace

"Plum Johnson upends every cliché about growing old in this prequel/sequel to her award-winning memoir, *They Left Us Everything*. This 'coming of age' story grabs you and shakes you up, catching you off guard as Plum takes the art of reinvention to new heights. I was enchanted by page seven, laughing out loud by page nine and hooked until the end. In love or business, Plum Johnson is her own high wire act, with humor often her only safety net. Forget Aesop, Brothers Grimm, or TV's *Golden Girls*: Plum's real-life cast is pure platinum."

—**Roxana Spicer, bestselling author of**
The Traitor's Daughter

"Plum Johnson is drawn to fairytales, yet at the same time wary because of their influence on the romantic choices she and many of us make. What's crystal clear, though, is that she is a writer who has no need of a Rumpelstiltskin figure to help her weave the complexities and complications of decades of lived experience—relationships both mistaken and enduring, work, art, homes, friendships, family—into story gold: a generous and often hilarious account of a woman's life eagerly and creatively lived."

—**Kathy Page, award-winning author of**
Dear Evelyn* and *In This Faulty Machine

"Plum Johnson is a natural storyteller, and what a tale she has to tell. Not a fairy tale but real life adventure, brimming with spirit, and full of the bruises, scrapes and glories that come from living courageously. What a treat to be along on this exciting ride and to watch our heroine blossom into seeing herself as the kickass queen she clearly has been all along."

—**Gill Deacon, bestselling author, journalist and podcaster**

Select Praise for *They Left Us Everything*

Winner of the 2015 RBC Taylor Prize

#1 NATIONAL BESTSELLER

"A poetic meditation on aging, grief and filial responsibility."
—*The Globe and Mail*

"At times heartbreaking and at others hysterically funny. . . . The book's descriptive prose brings [the] places and people to life and poignantly conveys the quasi-spiritual journey that helps Johnson overcome her grief." —*Publishers Weekly*

"Generous and heartfelt . . . an uplifting affirmation of human relationships and the cycle of life itself. A warmly candid memoir of navigating family, aging, and death." —*Kirkus Reviews*

"The kind of slim, unassuming memoir that hits you deep in the gut." —*National Post*

"Anyone who has packed up the family home after a parent's death will fall in love with this charming book. An all-too-human, funny, and poignant tale of saying goodbye."
—**Susan Swan, author of *Big Girls Don't Cry***

"An honest and revealing look at what makes an old family home more than just walls and a roof . . . [Johnson] exposes the complexity and connectivity of family relationships."
—**Iain Reid, author of *I'm Thinking of Ending Things***

"Johnson writes with clarity, wit and a powerful descriptive voice that makes the rambling family home she moves back into for 16 weeks a character in itself." —*NOW Toronto*

"A lovely memoir." —*Maclean's*

The Trouble
with Fairy Tales

ALSO BY PLUM JOHNSON

They Left Us Everything

The Trouble with
FAIRY TALES

A memoir

PLUM JOHNSON

VIKING

VIKING

an imprint of Penguin Canada, a division of Penguin Random House Canada Limited

Canada • USA • UK • Ireland • Australia • New Zealand • India • South Africa • China

First published 2025

Viking, an imprint of Penguin Canada
A division of Penguin Random House Canada
320 Front Street West, Suite 1400
Toronto, Ontario, M5V 3B6, Canada
penguinrandomhouse.ca

The authorized representative in the EU for product safety and compliance is Penguin Random House Ireland, Morrison Chambers, 32 Nassau Street, Dublin D02 YH68, Ireland, https://eu-contact.penguin.ie

This is a work of nonfiction. The names and identifying details of certain individuals and locations have been changed to protect their privacy.

The excerpt from Hafez on page 240 is from his poem "All the Hemispheres."

Photographs courtesy of the author unless otherwise noted.
Oakville Record-Star photograph by Charles Osland.

LIBRARY AND ARCHIVES CANADA CATALOGUING IN PUBLICATION

Title: The trouble with fairy tales : a memoir / Plum Johnson.
Names: Johnson, Plum, author
Identifiers: Canadiana (print) 20250170876 | Canadiana (ebook) 20250170884 |
ISBN 9780735250727 (softcover) | ISBN 9780735250710 (EPUB)
Subjects: LCSH: Johnson, Plum. | LCSH: Johnson, Plum—Childhood and youth. |
LCSH: Fairy tales—Psychological aspects. | LCSH: Creation (Literary, artistic, etc.)—
Psychological aspects. | LCSH: Authors, Canadian—21st century—Biography. |
LCSH: Women authors—21st century—Biography. | LCSH: Authors—
21st century—Biography. | LCGFT: Autobiographies.
Classification: LCC BF408 .J63 2025 | DDC 153.3/5092—dc23

Cover and book design by Kate Sinclair
Typeset in Baskerville by Sean Tai
Cover image courtesy of the author
Printed in Canada

10 9 8 7 6 5 4 3 2 1

Penguin
Random House
VIKING CANADA

The stories that I fashioned once are fairy tales, and they cannot satisfy me now.

Daphne du Maurier

TABLE OF CONTENTS

Courage My Love

🜍

PEARL'S HAIR SALON is a tiny place tucked around the side of an old four-story apartment building. It's within walking distance of my house in downtown Toronto, and for years I've been sneaking into Pearl's every month to have my roots touched up.

There are only three chairs facing the mirrors, and on busy days, Pearl darts between them like a hummingbird, multitasking to the ding of a timer. Sometimes young men come in for quick haircuts, but mostly it's women my age, other pensioners who appreciate Pearl's reasonable prices and the fact that her radio is always tuned to a soothing classical station. None of us minds the tired decor and the occasional blip when the air conditioner fails or the hot water inconveniently surges; we feel like a supportive community of like-minded souls, even though we're strangers. We do what women have always done in the intimacy of a beauty salon: We let down our hair—we confide and confess; we talk about love.

As Pearl slathers brown dye on my hair, I strike up a conversation with the woman sitting in the chair beside me. Her gray-blonde hair is already plastered with streaks of gooey bleach and folded strips of tinfoil stick out of her head like electrodes. We discover that we grew up in the same hometown and she's read my previous memoir, *They Left Us Everything.* Pearl knows all about that book, too, because when it won a prize, the shock caused bits of my hair to fall out.

"What are you writing about now?" the woman asks.

I never know how to answer this question when I'm struggling to write a new manuscript, so I just blurt out, "Old boyfriends!"

"Oh, I've got a few of those," she says, "only now they're *old* in more ways than one."

"Which fairy tales were they?"

"Fairy tales?"

"You know . . ." I say, "like Sleeping Beauty when you were first kissed awake . . . or some Pied Piper who led you astray. You must have been Little Red Riding Hood once, weren't you? Didn't you ever meet a wolf?"

"Oh yes," she says, nodding, "probably more than one."

"See? And how about Cinderella? Didn't you ever meet your prince?"

"Sure! Got married in my twenties, but it didn't work out so well."

"Same here." I shake my head. "So, what happened to us? How come we kept falling for fairy tales?"

"Blame the Brothers Grimm!" she says, laughing.

"Exactly! I keep thinking about all the messages we got—be good little girls . . . stay on the path . . . wait to be rescued . . . one day your prince will come. Do you think we were *groomed*?"

"*Doomed*?" She fiddles with the cotton in her ears.

"Well, maybe that too." I point to the celebrity magazine she's flipping through. "Have you ever watched *The Bachelor* . . . or *Say Yes to the Dress*? We're still buying this shit!"

Just then, Pearl's timer dings. As she leads me over to the basin to lather shampoo through my hair, a lyric from *South Pacific* cascades through my ears. How many times have I tried to wash that man out of my hair? How many times have I sacrificed myself to romance? Postponed my dreams? Lost myself in a man? It was only once I'd left a man that I found myself again.

Pearl hands me a towel.

"You know what fairy tale I'm starring in now?" I say, clipping my hair back.

"No, what?"

"The Traveling Musicians—it's the one where a bunch of animals are told they're too old to be useful, so they're abandoned in the woods and left to die."

"That sounds like me," she says. "I used to live in a big house, but when my husband left me, we had to sell it. I live alone in a seniors' residence now. My children want me to wear an alarm in case I drown in the tub or fall over the balcony. It makes them feel better, but I hate it." She smiles. "At least it's not a nursing home . . . yet."

"Well, there's no nursing home in The Traveling Musicians! When the old animals meet each other, they decide to band together and create a whole new adventure. They reinvent themselves."

I remind her of a modern film version: *The Best Exotic Marigold Hotel*. It's no wonder that movie was such a blockbuster hit with the boomer generation.

"Good luck with your book," she calls out as I'm leaving. "Make sure there's lots of romance and drama."

"Drama?"

She giggles. "Sure! Everyone likes to read about romance and drama. You should see what goes on in my apartment building!"

LEAVING PEARL'S, I HOP THE streetcar and make my way down to Kensington Market. It's a gritty part of the city where fishmongers and fruit stands spill onto the sidewalks and painted Victorian houses sell secondhand clothing and bongs. Winding my way through the crowded streets, past stores with names like *Breathless* and *Exile*, I arrive at *Courage My Love*. It's the vintage shop where I often go to rescue orphaned dresses that remind me of my youth. I keep hoping to stumble upon my old prom dress, a short piece of pale-pink fluff with spaghetti straps that I wore to a cadet ball in 1963. It would be fun to run into the cadet who took me (I think his name was Floyd), but I'm much more interested in reuniting with that dress. I wonder what happened to it?

Outside the shop I thumb through their circular racks twirling with crinolines and ancient fur coats, then trip up the steps piled with old boots. Inside, I'm enthralled with the shelves of my past. Above glass-topped counters cluttered with hippie beads, incense and Mexican silver, I spy patent leather handbags, ceramic Bambi lamps and souvenir ashtrays from Niagara Falls. There's even an Elvis bust.

As I riffle through treasures from the fifties and sixties— tiny-waisted cocktail dresses, circular poodle skirts—I'm thinking, *Why aren't old women treated like treasures?* After all, we're pre-loved and meet the definition of vintage: We're at least twenty years older than everyone else. Some of us are mid-century modern, some prewar, some even qualify as antique—like my good friend Pat, for example, who's in her mid-nineties. She bewitched me when I was seven years old by teaching me art in grade 2; now she's my oldest living friend. I call her my "Other Mother."

Suddenly, in the lingerie section, I spy a floor-length swish of red-hot silk—somebody else's long-lost memory— and quickly buy it for forty dollars. It's missing its sleeves, but the neckline is adorned with crushed velvet petals, and the operatic resonance of it makes me feel like singing arias all the way home.

Tonight, I slip it over my blue jeans and T-shirt and invite my friend Les to come for a drink. It's after nine o'clock. Most of my other friends are asleep by now, but I can always count on Les. She keeps artist's hours, working into the night like I do, and her husband doesn't seem to mind. For almost twenty years, we've been sharing our thoughts, reading aloud, facing our fears, propping each other up.

Just before she arrives, I rummage in the box under my bed where I keep my old shoes and stick my pedicured toes into lacy, pink mules—absurdly high, extravagant heels I haven't worn in twenty years, not since a certain lover slept over. It takes so little to feel sexy again. Gripping the banister, I teeter cautiously down the staircase, careful not to trip on my new wings of silk as they flutter dangerously behind me.

"I love coming to your house," says Les, waving her arms around my front hall. "It's so artistic!"

I recognize the word *artistic* as friend-speak for clutter. Books are strewn everywhere, overflowing from shelves and stacked on the floor. Unfinished paintings lean against walls, and an antique, wool bathing suit dangles from a standing lamp. In the fridge, bottles of nail polish are nestled in the egg compartment, and whenever I go to get ice cubes, old paintbrushes wrapped in plastic bags to keep them pliable tumble out of the freezer. Forty years ago, when my three children were young, their friends said they felt so free here, mistaking the chaos for anarchy. "At least you'll be safe from burglars," quipped my brother Victor, "because who would break in, when every room looks ransacked already?"

Back then, as a single mother, when I had more imagination than money, I'd "renovated" my kitchen by mirroring all the walls. I told everyone it was to create the illusion of distance and space, but the real purpose was to see myself reflected into infinity to prove that I still existed. Now, when Les walks in, she sees the mirrors are covered with yellow sticky notes.

"Is this how you're writing now," she says, looking around, "using your mirrors as a bulletin board?"

"I've been rearranging those all week," I say, "trying to find my theme."

"I like this one!" She points to a note near the ceiling where I've written in big block letters: WHO AM I?

"That's my biggest question!"

"It's our *universal* question." Les plonks her elbows on the counter to watch me make coffee. "Who am I now . . . and who was I then?"

"I can't figure it out," I shout over the hissing of the espresso machine. "How do we ever make sense of our lives when there are so many threads to untangle?"

"You can't tie your life into a tidy bow," says Les, tugging at her gray corkscrew curls. "It's always going to be a straggly, messy, untidy thing."

"But what did it all mean? They say if you don't know where you're going, you'll end up someplace else. But which of us ever knew where we were going? And now that we're here—at this someplace else—how did we get here?"

"Exactly. We're baffled. Old age has happened so fast."

"My friend Pat says you can only know yourself through *relationship* . . . but in every relationship, I've been a different person."

"How many relationships have you had?"

"I can't remember! Sometimes I think I can . . . and then one night I'm lying in the bathtub, and I think, *Oh! I forgot about him!*"

Les laughs. "Me too . . . but I remember what his shoes looked like."

"So how can we truly know ourselves?"

"That's the thing. We may never know."

"But I knew who I was when I was *eight*—didn't you? I was inventing products, producing plays . . . I'd even written my first book by then. Then something happened, and I lost my way! How do we drift so far away from our childhood dreams, from what we were meant to do?"

"Hormones!" says Les.

"Really? It's that simple?"

"Sure! Don't you remember how mesmerizing boys were? How alluring love was? When puberty strikes, we abandon ourselves."

I switch on the tiny, white fairy lights that snake around my kitchen window, then light a candle and carry it outside to the patio table. Low in the sky, a summer moon hovers. We can hear the radio in the kitchen faintly playing jazz.

"Remember how we felt at seventeen?" Les says, collapsing into a wrought iron chair. "We felt so wild, so full of passion. There was such a long road ahead, like anything was possible!"

She starts to sing "Try to Remember" and the wind lifts her notes into the wistful rustle of the trees. For three glorious hours, we sit outside in the glow of the candle, sharing stories of our misspent youth, laughing like conspiring rebels at the absurdity of it. By then we're feeling totally reckless—drinking espresso, and it's not even decaf.

The trouble happens later, after Les leaves, after the caffeine has kept me awake all night, when the pain in my lower back from the high heels means I can't walk for two days.

Still, it was worth it.

Despite what I look like on the outside—the sagging skin and gnarled arthritic joints—on the inside I feel thirty-two. Les says she feels twenty-eight. Pat recently told me she feels forty-five, even though she's ninety-five. We all have a young person locked inside, as if the clock had stopped, each of us channeling our best age, when we felt on top of the world. The passions we felt in our youth continue to flicker and ferment below the surface, waiting to be reignited, often erupting as fierce as ever, sometimes even more so.

The reality is that my knob-and-tube wiring is too old to replace. Barnacles have started to appear on my back. I find myself worrying about weather forecasts and the rising price of gasoline just like my mother did, and I carefully clutch railings as I descend subway stairs, my pockets full of tissues now, to dab at my eyes when the wind blows. The third finger on my right hand is often locked when I wake in the morning, so I pry it open using the edge of my mattress.

I used to use my mattress for other things.

I have no wish to compete with the young: to inject Botox, lift my face, or ingest hormones to embrace a man on Viagra. Somebody needs to show the younger generation what old age looks like. It might as well be me.

On the other hand, maybe we should all wear T-shirts emblazoned with photos of our younger selves to remind others what we used to look like. We all looked gorgeous then, we just didn't appreciate it. These days, whenever I look in the mirror, I try to remind myself that I'll never look younger than I do today. At seventy-seven, my wrinkles are coming along just fine, delicate crisscrossed lines that look like crushed silk, the kind I always wanted, and I'm glad I no longer care so much about the shape of my eyebrows. I'm happy to embrace my interior landscape, to spend my time thinking, assessing, looking back at the forks in the road, sometimes with regret, but mostly with curiosity, trying to make sense of the choices I made—searching for meaning.

What were the themes of my life, my failings, my plot? All good stories take shape. Some look like waves that build to crescendos, others like steps to the top of a mountain. It feels like I've been swept out to sea every seven years or so, but I've also plunged off a few cliffs. Perhaps mine wasn't one long journey. Perhaps I've lived many short stories all strung together.

So, why am I still rearranging those sticky notes?

It's because I'm avoiding a story that needs to be told.

ONCE UPON A TIME, I thought this memoir would be a walk in the park. I thought I could just take my basket and skip through the woods—tra-la-la—following crumbs down memory lane all the way back to Granny's house. But I hear a growl in the bushes; the hairs on the back of my neck stand up. Is it possible that all my romantic adventures had elements of a fairy tale? How is this possible when I was raised in the twentieth century . . . *by a feminist?*

I go to my bookcase and take out *The Blue Fairy Book*, the one I remember from childhood. Mum must have thought it was harmless; it was hers before mine, and Granny's before hers, originally published in 1889. It used to sit by my bedside luring me in with its gold-embossed cover and secretive etchings, the first one hiding behind a thin veil of tissue. Peeling back the veil was like opening a magic door.

By the time I've connected my real-life enchantments to that small, gilded book, I realize I've traipsed through so many tropes—romantic clichés from Cinderella, The Pied Piper, Rapunzel and more—enthralled by the drama of it all. How many other young girls were seduced by these scripts? Even the costumes—the peasant blouse, dirndl and clogs; the ball gowns, girdles and gloves; the aprons, slippers and rags—I think I've owned them all.

Nobody really knows where fairy tales originated. They've been circulating for thousands of years in almost every culture on earth, embedded by now in the bedrock of our psyches, their plots metastasizing into every soap opera ever produced.

I like to think they originated with women, generations of old wives who'd already lived them, who knew a thing or two about the frailties of human nature, women who whispered their stories to each other as they hung their washing and waited on shore for their men to return from sea. They probably hoped to warn us . . . and I should have paid closer attention. But since when do any of us learn from history? We don't even listen to our mothers.

Instead, I frolicked through my roles without much care for the consequences. I expected to "let down my hair" or be "kissed awake" and carried away by a prince who would cut through brambles to reach me. He'd throw off his cloak, kneel at my feet and declare his undying love. I'd learned, of course, that he'd come disguised as a beggar (or was it a frog . . . or a beast?) and reveal himself once I kissed him. My love would fix and restore him . . . if only I loved him enough. But later, in real life, a plot twist would shock me: A prince might turn into a beggar, or a frog into Bluebeard—it was all so confusing—yet most of the time I hung in there, still thinking I was doing Cinderella. Some princes hung around all my life, even after the slipper didn't fit, they—or I—holding a torch that never quite quit and becoming instead, "the one who got away."

The trouble with fairy tales is that they're *not true*, yet they weave in and out of our hopes and dreams, fueling our fantasies for the rest of our lives. Why didn't we ask what happened *next*? What happened to Little Red Riding Hood after she was rescued by the woodcutter? Or to Cinderella after she married the prince? Because "happily ever after" is never "the end" . . . life always gives us more chapters.

The Path to Granny's House

LET ME TELL YOU a family fairy tale . . .

Long before I was born, my British granny died in the ex-pat community of Oporto, Portugal. She died in 1917 at the age of forty-two, leaving behind five children. Her youngest—my father—had just turned two years old. She died of dropsy (a romantic-sounding word that reminded me of *curtsy*) and was buried in the graveyard of the Anglican Church of St. James. I knew nothing much else about her.

After her death, my grandfather, a well-to-do merchant, quickly married his secretary, a conniving young woman who then issued a cruel ultimatum: "It's me or your children— you can't have both!" I imagine her delivering this speech in her wedding dress, before smashing her bouquet at his feet. (Was she really conniving? Or did her new stepchildren put words in her mouth? I can only relay what I heard from my aunt.)

A few weeks later, in the elegant dining room of their quinta overlooking the River Douro where his fleet of ships was moored, Grandfather summoned his children (Dad remembered being in his high chair) and announced his decision: He was banishing them across the English Channel to a rented house in Brighton where he'd arranged for them to be raised by a friend named Miss Alice.

Seventeen-year-old George was enraged. Knocking over his chair, he raced upstairs to his bedroom and returned with a pistol. He aimed at his wicked young stepmother and cocked it. But just as he fired, his younger brother Charles leapt up and knocked the gun from his hand, causing the shot to go through the ceiling. Having missed his target, George fainted. Grandfather had his limp body carried down the hill to the harbor and thrown onto one of his ships destined for Canada. In Halifax, young George hopped a train for Alberta, became a farmer and rarely saw his siblings again. Charles went out to work and the youngest children moved to Brighton.

But karma circled back, and Grandfather's import-export business soon ran into trouble. In 1929, a violent earthquake struck off the coast of Newfoundland, creating a tsunami of such force that giant waves hit the coast at forty kilometers per hour, wrecking what remained of his shipping fleet. (His schooner *The Edith M. Cavell* lies sunken off the coast to this day.) That's when Grandfather discovered his ships were uninsured. His young wife, in cahoots with his unscrupulous business manager, had pocketed the premiums instead of paying them. After they ran off, Grandfather died of a heart attack, bankrupt.

In Brighton, the children were orphaned and marooned. Creditors arrived at their rented house, shoved Miss Alice aside, removed everything of value and turfed them out. Without any means of support, what was Miss Alice to do? She took in washing to make ends meet and loved those children for the rest of her life as if they were her own.

Dad called her "Ar." The mists of time have swallowed the origins of her nickname. Perhaps as a toddler, Dad heard his older siblings call her "our," as in "our new mother." Even Dad couldn't remember. But he kept Ar's photo on his dresser to the end of his days.

Now, I may have embellished this tale over time, or even fabricated bits out of whole cloth, but the details don't really matter. All you need to remember is that there was—programmed into my subconscious—this family fairy tale of a widowed father, motherless children . . . and a fairy godmother who came to their rescue.

Every Saturday morning, as I watched Dad polish Ar's small, silver picture frame, I wished I could be her—the woman Dad worshipped.

I forgot Mum's warning: *Be careful what you wish for . . .*

———

IN 1946, THE YEAR I WAS BORN, World War II had ended in Europe and Mum had come home to her family's farm in Virginia as a pregnant war bride to give birth to me. Only two years earlier, she'd been a U.S. Army sergeant, working for the American Red Cross at a fighter base in England, where she'd married Dad, a Royal Navy lieutenant. He received news of my birth by telegram aboard ship in the Pacific because Dad's war wasn't finished yet. He was still mopping up operations in the Far East.

When I was six months old, Mum took me to Hong Kong to meet Dad for the first time. By then he had rejoined his previous company as an insurance executive and purchased a plot of land high up on The Peak, where he set about building our house. Meanwhile, we lived in splendor at the Repulse Bay Hotel, surrounded by staff. I was dressed in organdy sundresses with starched, pink ribbons in my pale-blonde hair and carried on the back of my amah while Mum played mahjong with other ex-pat wives in an arched veranda off the hotel lobby. In photographs of my first birthday, I'm seen sticking my thumb in a cake adorned with sugarplums, surrounded by adults laughing and smoking, all dressed in cocktail attire. Every child seated at the long banquet table has a Chinese amah in a starched white tunic standing behind them.

Mum gave birth to my brother Sandy a year later. I have only a smattering of memories from this early time—a time of confusion, impending upheaval and a gathering fear of loss. We seemed to be always moving. Two years later, we moved to Singapore, where my brother Robin was born.

Mum had always been adventurous, but she tired of the idle ex-pat life, the endless tennis and mahjong games and dealing with the damp heat and mildew. She could see a new storm of political unrest gathering in the region and she wanted to be back in secure, familiar surroundings. She missed her family. In December 1950, she got word that her mother was seriously ill in America and gave Dad an ulti-matum: Book flights home, or she'd do it herself. When he ignored her demand, she defiantly scooped up the three of us and left Dad behind—a pattern I would unconsciously repeat thirty years later. She was thirty-four years old.

We arrived back at the family farm in Virginia just in time to see her mother, who died shortly after. Rokeby Farm sat on a hill, overlooking three hundred and fifty acres of fertile land on the outskirts of Fredericksburg. It was origi-nally bought by Mum's father as a weekend retreat from his life as a banker in Richmond. It had been a summer home for his wife and eight children, but during the Great Depression, his bank failed and he died of a heart attack when Mum was fifteen. It was now a working farm, run by my uncle, but it was mostly a house full of women—my mother, two aunts and four older female cousins slept down the hall.

At the farm, I felt like an outsider. Despite all the people around, I felt lonely and confused. I missed Daddy. Gone was my precious amah, Ah Khan. Instead, tall, large-boned aunts wearing hats and white gloves descended on the farm to fuss over me. The staccato chatter of people's voices had melted to a liquid drawl. There were no monkeys, no palm trees.

In the fall of 1951, my first day at nursery school coincided with Halloween, a celebration I knew nothing about. In an early morning rush, Mum took me down to the farmhouse cellar and pulled old clothes from a musty trunk. She dressed me in a long cotton skirt, a knitted shawl and an itchy yellow eye mask made of starched gauze. We drove into town in the wood-paneled station wagon and entered a room full of small, masked strangers.

"Be good," said Mum, giving me a kiss. After she left, the teacher lifted me onto a big table in the middle of the room for all to see and said in a loud voice, "Who are you?"

When I didn't answer, she said, "Who are you trying to be?"

Who was I? Who was I trying to be? I didn't know. I stood there silently, looking down at all the scary faces, and slowly wet my pants. I tried not to cry, but hot tears of humiliation trickled out, dissolving the starch and sticking the mask to my face.

Dad finally returned in December. In the middle of a Christmas party, someone bent down, pointed towards the front door and said, "See? Over there! Your daddy's come!" Everyone rushed to hug him, but I held back. He'd been gone almost a quarter of my lifetime and the only thing I recognized was his hat.

The following January, in 1952, we emigrated to Canada. We said goodbye to the farm in Virginia and drove north, crossing the border at Fort Erie. Dad called it "pioneering." The New Zealand Insurance Company had asked him to open their Canadian branch in Toronto.

We settled in Oakville, a small, semi-rural town with fewer than six thousand people on the shores of Lake Ontario that was close enough to Toronto that Dad could commute to work. Property at the time was less expensive than the city, so the town attracted artists and entrepreneurs and new immigrants. Mum fell in love with a barn of a house that had no furnace and no insulation, but it had a warm embrace and a limitless horizon facing the lake. A weeping willow bent over the pebbly beach and purple lilacs crowned the dirt path.

The war had been over for six years, and all around us, people were rebuilding their lives and making up for lost time. Fathers left for work early in the morning, often taking the only family car, and didn't return until suppertime. Many of the mothers, once working girls with college degrees, were now reined in and leashed to the kitchen sink with toddlers underfoot. Mum made friends with other mothers—writers, sculptors, painters and weavers, all of them clinging to their artistic expression for sanity. One night a week they met under clandestine cover, sometimes to sculpt at Dinny Young's studio down by the pier, sometimes to paint in Nan Wilkes's kitchen. I was too young to

understand Mum's frustrations and motivations, I just heard
the explosions when Dad found out, when he grabbed her
artwork and flung it in the fire, shouting that she should have
been home, washing the dishes.

One Saturday in our new house, I was upstairs with
Mum. She was writing letters at the desk in her dressing
room and gave me some paper so I could write too. I sat on
the carpet and drew stories about a little mouse who lived
in a hat and got carried around the world without anybody
knowing he was there. When I finished, Mum paper-clipped
my three pages together and said, "There! You've written
a book!" Since I'd already been carried around the world
myself, I suppose it was my autobiography, but it was drawn,
not written. I didn't understand why grown-up books weren't
full of pictures like mine, but when I asked Mum why, she
didn't know either. I looked across the room to Mum's bedside table, where the book *Maria and The Captain*, written
by her best friend, Isabel Dunn, sat on top. Suddenly I knew
that one day a book of mine would sit there too. I don't
know how I knew. I just saw it there.

Outside in the garden, Daddy was pushing his lawn
mower. A breeze from the lake fluttered through the window
screen, and I could smell the sweet, fresh grass and the odor
of rotting seaweed from the beach beyond. A shaft of mid-
morning light streamed through the window. Strange gray
specks were dancing in it.

"Dust motes," said Mum.

But I knew that's not what they were. They were me in the past, me in the future, all of us—our flakes. One day I knew I'd dance in the sun again, like those.

"Are souls used over and over again?" I asked Mum.

She looked up from her writing with one eyebrow raised. "What on earth made you ask me that?"

Whenever my brothers and I cuddled up to Mum for a bedtime story and shouted, "Tell us a story that *really* happened!" she'd tell us a ghost story. Usually, she told us about Marmion, an historic plantation in Virginia near where she grew up. She said the south was "riddled" with ghosts.

"We used to go to dances at Marmion," she'd say. "Daddy would take us in his Packard, and all the cousins would spend the night."

"Where did you sleep?"

"There was a big room they turned into a dormitory for the girls."

"And there was a ghost there?" we'd prompt, wide-eyed (we'd heard this story before).

"Yes! The ghost of Marmion! A sweet young girl from the 1700s. She'd come down the stairs in her long, blue nightgown and . . ."

"Warn all the travelers!" we'd shout in unison.

"That's right!"

"Did you ever see her?"

"No, darling, I never did. But Aunt Emily saw her once. Aunt Gittie did, too, and she was *a doctor*, so I never doubted her account."

"What did she say the ghost looked like?"

"She had long, blonde hair in a braid down her back. Little white slippers, I think."

"Weren't people scared?"

"Oh, no! She never did any harm. She came to *save* people."

"Who did she save?" This was the part of Mum's story that always changed, the part we could hardly wait for her to get to.

"Well . . . one time it was Uncle Ennion. He was supposed to go riding the next morning. But she told him not to go. So, he didn't. He slept in . . . and you know what?"

"What? What?!"

"A big lightning storm came up the valley! All the trees came crashing down! He would have been killed if he'd gone riding in that."

All of Mum's ghost stories involved premonitions and warnings. "All ghosts are benign," she'd say, as if to reassure us.

Ghosts loomed large in my imagination because a block away from our house there was a huge Victorian funeral home that resembled a castle, complete with turrets and stained glass windows. The owners had two young sons who befriended my brothers and often snuck them into what they claimed was the embalming room in the basement. They'd return with fantastical reports of dark, winding tunnels, gruesome body parts and channels of spurting blood. I knew they were probably making all of this up, but still I pictured ghosts escaping out the windows, floating away like smoke from the eaves.

Across the road from the funeral home, on the property that abutted our garden, was a large coach house that had once housed horse-drawn carriages. It was owned by Miss Amice Calverley, an eccentric Egyptologist with clouds of gray hair who wore big, flapping garments. She had divided the ground floor into rented flats, where some of the bedrooms were still wood-framed horse stalls, and she lived upstairs in one of the lofts. Even though she was only in her mid-fifties when I was five, I considered her ancient. Initially, I gave her a wide berth, hiding behind Mum's skirts when she dropped in for a visit, but soon a shy friendship developed between us. She'd recently moved back from Egypt, where she'd been funded by John D. Rockefeller to record the reliefs of the great temple of Seti I at Abydos. Now she was transcribing her field sketches into large colored illustrations, bound into giant portfolios destined for the University of Chicago, and she began inviting me up to her studio. While I played quietly on the floor with her set of ivory pick-up sticks, she'd occasionally hand me her magnifying glass so I could see the tiny feathers she'd just inked onto an owl. Sometimes she took a break and played her antique piano. She claimed her dog could play duets, and he'd sit beside her with his paws on the keyboard, howling out the window.

One day, she said, "Stay here, while I feed Mr. Manley." I watched out the window as she carried a bucket of water to the tall furry walnut tree at the bottom of her garden. I knew this meant she could talk to trees and my heart burst with admiration—all her trees had names.

In the fall, I began grade 1 at Miss Lightbourn's School for Girls. It was a small school within walking distance, held in a residential home surrounded by a white picket fence. Miss Lightbourn was tall and spindly, always smiling kindly with gold-rimmed teeth. When she walked, she swayed slightly, like a giraffe. The large public high school was one block north, so for the next seven years, we watched those students saunter past, hooting and jeering at us as we did our calisthenics in the playground dressed in our tunics and navy-blue bloomers. Sometimes, we'd arrive in the morning to find mysterious four-letter words splashed in black paint across our fence. Miss Lightbourn wouldn't complain or explain what the words meant, she'd just hand us buckets of soapy water and brushes and supervise while we removed the graffiti. She believed in "turning the other cheek." To her, the most important subjects in school were religious studies and gardening, so she taught those herself. Every spring, she gave each class a small patch of the playground to cultivate with seeds and judged the best garden at the end of June, on prize day. My class spent every recess thinking up ways to win the prize. I wanted to plant dandelions, because they were always the first ones up. I loved to weave their yellow blossoms into necklaces and watch how they changed into balls of fluff that blew in the wind and traveled far away. But everyone said, "No, no, you can't grow *weeds*!"

I asked Dad, "Why are dandelions called weeds? Why aren't poppies called weeds? Or marigolds?"

"Weeds are flowers that grow in the wrong place," he said.

This was something I didn't understand. Who decided where the wrong place was? I pondered this as we drove past beautiful goldenrods waving their tails beside the highway, and I pondered this on Sundays when we ran down the hill to St. Jude's church and sat in the back pew. Harry Foster sat beside us, jotting down notes from the sermon on the back of his leaflet. He owned a big advertising agency and was planning to start the Special Olympics with Rose Kennedy.

At the end of grade 1, Miss Lightbourn gave me the Proficiency Award, a picture book about the coronation of Queen Elizabeth II. After grade 2, she accelerated me, putting me in a room where grades 3 and 4 were taught together. The new teacher taught us that rocks were "inanimate." She said, "Inanimate objects don't breathe, change or live." I remember staring at her, astonished. Didn't she know that rocks were living things? Did she think they'd never been born? Didn't breathe? Wouldn't change? One day, I thought, everyone will learn the language of rocks, just like Miss Calverley already knew the language of trees. In fact, our art teacher, Pat Goss, often took us into the nearby park to draw trees and said that if we observed them closely, we'd see that "each tree has its own personality."

———

OVER THE NEXT FEW YEARS, Mum had two more babies. Each time, Dad came running into our bedrooms early in the morning, throwing open our curtains and shouting, "It's a boy! It's a boy!" He was so excited, he wanted us all to dress quickly so he could drive us to the hospital to look through the window while Mum held the baby up to the glass. I groaned, thinking, *Not another boy*, and put my head in the pillow. All I wanted was *a sister*.

Mum had always told us the lake was a dangerous place. She told us never to go close to the edge of the water, to stay on the safe path above it. The next time I had a friend over, I kept my promise. Brenda and I were whooping it up, little sharpshooters in bare feet, racing along the path, rehearsing for our Annie Oakley rodeo. Brenda loved to gallop, so she always played the horse. I was trying to lasso some branches.

Suddenly a man appeared from behind the bushes, dressed in a suit and tie. He smiled and we smiled, and then he said, "Come, let me show you something special behind this tree." What happened next, I could never fully describe, not even in court.

We weren't rescued by a woodcutter; we were rescued by a neighbor who lived nearby. She stumbled upon the scene and alerted my mother, who called the police. I heard Mum say, "What? They caught him?! Oh, thank God."

At the local police station, a tall policeman held my hand and walked me down a narrow corridor where five men were standing in a lineup with their backs to the wall. He asked me to reach out and touch the man's sleeve. This was far scarier than seeing him on the path and I had nightmares after that. Whenever the wind blew and the branches of the maple tree tapped on my bedroom window at night, I was sure I could see his face—he was a wolf!

The day of the trial, Mum and Dad drove me to the courthouse. Brenda and I were brought in separately to testify. I was first, and the courthouse reminded me of church. I could see Mum and Dad in the front pew. A policeman walked me up the aisle and helped me climb up into the pulpit.

At a long oak table cluttered with papers, the wolf sat between two lawyers. His thin, sad-looking wife sat on the bench behind them, wearing a powder-blue dress and a small navy hat. She was weeping into her hanky, and I couldn't take my eyes off her. During the testimony, we learned they were Swedish immigrants with three small children at home.

"Now," the prosecutor said to me, "would you please describe to the court what this man did?" There was complete silence. I looked at Mum. She nodded in encouragement.

"Tell us what he did," repeated the prosecutor.

"He . . . um . . . he undid his zipper," I whispered, feeling my face getting hot. I could hear the man's wife sobbing.

"Yes? And then?"

"He undid his zipper," I whispered again.

"Yes, yes," said the prosecutor. "He undid his zipper. *Then* what did he do? Please, speak up!"

I looked down at my lap and back up at the sad woman sobbing into her hanky, and thought, *What will happen to her if the wolf is sent away to jail? Who will feed her and her children?* I knew what he showed me was bad, but was it that bad? After all, I had little brothers. I'd seen one before.

"I don't know."

"You don't know?"

I shook my head.

"So, that's all this man did? He simply undid his zipper?"

The prosecutor looked exasperated with me. I was afraid to look at Mum and Dad, afraid to see their disappointment. The person I wanted to rescue was the wolf's wife.

"You may step down," said the judge. "Go sit with your parents."

Just then, the two big wooden doors at the back of the courtroom creaked open and Brenda strutted in. She sashayed down the aisle like a movie star. The policeman wasn't holding her hand, he was trailing along behind her. In a loud, accusatory voice, she described exactly what the man did on our lakefront path. When she said the word *penis* out loud, I slid down in my pew, wishing I could be as brave as Brenda. After gasps from the onlookers and clucking of tongues, she waltzed over and sat down beside her parents, grinning ear to ear like she'd just won a spelling bee.

I LONGED TO GROW UP—tall enough to reach the peanut butter shelf and tall enough to see the top of Mum's bedroom dresser, which sparkled with silver brushes and crystal pots, her glitzy brooches sticking out of a pincushion beside her golden tube of lipstick. I was forbidden to touch those feminine things. They belonged to a curious world of women's make-believe that I didn't understand: the intoxicating waft of Mum's perfume before she and Dad left for a cocktail party, her sparkly earrings, her pale-green satin dress, her bright-red fingernails—as if she was all dressed up for her role in a play. She seemed happy to entrust me with the care of my brothers (during the day, I was her number one babysitter), but I sensed from the way she whispered with her gaggle of friends that there were "sisterhood secrets" she wouldn't share with me. I knew all about boys from my brothers, but I longed for a sister.

At school, I heard older girls whispering mysteriously about "flying up" to Girl Guides. I wasn't sure what it meant, but I thought it had something to do with growing up quickly by flying through a porthole. I wanted to "fly up," too, but they giggled and said that first I needed to suffer through Brownies.

Mum bought me a secondhand Brownie uniform and I was inducted as a Sprite. Every week, I rode my bike to a small wooden hut on Randall Street where we sat crosslegged on the floor while Brown Owl blew her whistle and read the rules. We needed to earn small felt patches for things like housekeeping, cooking and sewing. I'd already earned two: one embroidered with a picture of a broom and one with a saucepan, but I still needed the one for sewing. Everyone else was sewing aprons and shoe bags, but I had a better idea—and I knew just where to find the right fabric.

Up in my bedroom, I carefully laid my Brownie uniform flat on the floor. Using Dad's big scissors, I chopped the whole thing in half at the waist. Then I sliced off the sleeves, fringed all the edges, and threaded elastic through the skirt. After strapping on my holster, I grabbed my pearl-handled cap gun, popped on my cowgirl hat and ran down to show Mum. She was sitting at the dining room table, deep in thought, working on her column called Borderlines. She was hoping to sell it to an American newspaper to explain to their readers what was happening in Canada.

"What on earth?!" she said as I twirled around in my new fringed vest and skirt. "Oh, Annie Oakley!" She started clapping and laughing. "It's perfectly wonderful! *Wonderful!*"

As I raced along Randall Street, I could only imagine how proud Brown Owl would be. I already knew where I'd attach my sewing patch—right over the heart of my new vest like a sheriff's star! But when I banged open the old wooden door, I heard a collective intake of breath from all the little Brownies sitting in a circle. Brown Owl was speechless. When she finally came to her senses, she blew spit through her whistle and kicked me out of the pack.

"Never mind," said Mum when I arrived home in tears. "It just proves that most people have no imagination!"

Now I knew I'd never fly through the porthole. Why couldn't I be like other girls? I wanted to fit in, but I didn't know how.

But just when I thought I'd never have a sister, eight-year-old Diana moved in around the corner and became the friend I'd always wanted. She loved to invent things just like I did, and together we built an entrepreneurial empire. Over the next three years, we created a gold mine in the sandy crawl space under the house, an outdoor restaurant in the garden, and a detective agency and a lending library in the playroom. But our biggest achievement was our theater. In a thrilling phase of collaboration, we retreated down the rickety wooden stairs to the concrete cellar and began writing one-act plays based on fairy tales. All our spare time was spent painting backdrops, designing costumes and memorizing lines. On my ninth birthday, Dad told me to look under my bed. In his workshop, he'd secretly made me a set of footlights, shaped like an extra-long wooden flower box with a plug at one end. They were miraculous, as if we'd graduated to the big time. Whenever we needed a prop, Mum said, "Just make it!" It didn't matter what it was. "Mum! Mum! We need a spinning wheel!" "Just make it!"

One day a letter arrived from my mother's wealthy older brother in New York City. His wife had recently died, and Uncle Langbourne wrote that he was sending me an assortment of his late wife's belongings to use as costumes. Uncle Langbourne was almost mythical in our family, a tall, imposing figure who'd never had children and lived a rarified life apart from the rest of the family. As a young man during the Great Depression, he'd saved his father's bank from bankruptcy and become the family's hero. After World War II, he assisted with the Marshall Plan for the reconstruction of Europe and became a member of President Kennedy's advisory council. Everyone looked up to him for advice, including Dad.

Mum and I walked to the post office to collect the cardboard box. It was so big it took two of us to carry it back home. Inside were beautiful turn-of-the-century gowns made of silk organza with corseted bodices and delicate ruffles strewn with seed pearls. Some had little silk sacks of dried cork sewn under the armpits to absorb the sweat. There were even some professionally made costumes that Aunt Elizabeth and her neighborhood friends used as children when they performed plays in their parents' home in 1915. Inside the pocket of Robin Hood's red cape, we found an original playbill listing Nelson Rockefeller as Allen-a-Dale when he was only seven years old.

Mum rifled through the accessories—wigs, feathered headbands, silk stockings and velvet, fur-trimmed boots— and found a few small red leather boxes. They had Elizabeth's initials on top. "How odd," she murmured as she snapped open each one. One tiny art deco lipstick, decorated with diamonds and rubies, dangled from a ring. Mum whistled and shook her head. "This can't be right," she said. "I wonder why Langbourne sent you these?" Then she laughed and tossed the boxes to me.

Diana and I were entranced. We dreamt up new plots for the old costumes and began rehearsing our newest play, based on the fairy tale The Princess Who Never Cried. I played the king, Diana played the princess and we put wigs on my brothers and cast them as courtiers. When the prince came to visit, Diana cut up an onion onstage so she'd cry real tears. We rigged up a photo of Queen Elizabeth on a pulley so it fell from the ceiling before the curtain opened, and we made all the children in the audience stand up and sing "God Save the Queen."

Our theater company so expanded my imagination that the time seemed to span decades, but in reality it lasted only three years until Diana and her family moved away. Down came the shower curtain, along with the picture of the queen, and I carefully packed the beautiful costumes into a box, which I stored upstairs in my bedroom closet. Dad reclaimed our props department as the space where he polished his shoes. I mourned the loss of the theater and my best friend, and developed a niggling pain in my side, which only grew stronger as time passed. It turned out to be my appendix—that strange little pouch attached to our gut that seems to have no purpose, except to burst and inflict pain.

I was soon rushed to the local hospital for an emergency appendectomy, after which an infection set in. I overheard Dr. Soanes telling Mum in the doorway that my condition was serious. He came over to my bed, clinked down the metal railing and sat on my sheets, his kindly shoulders slumped. He was holding a coil of thin clear tubing and told me I'd have to be brave. I could tell from Mum's expression that she already knew of some impending horror; she was steeling herself, preparing to be an accomplice. As her hands held me down, I fought and gagged and struggled for breath, while the tubing was shoved up my nose, down my throat and into my abdomen. Then I passed out.

When I awoke, I was trapped in a web of tubing. The tube from my nose looped up to my forehead, where it was taped between my eyes. I could see the poisonous yellow pus bubbling out through the clear plastic, making soft gurgling noises as it snaked over to a machine at my side. My right arm was strapped to a board, where another tube pumped antibiotics into my vein. For days, my temperature remained dangerously high with the raging infection.

Mum came to visit every afternoon. Whenever my eyes flickered open, I could see her sitting beside my bed, anxiety etched on her face. "Please get well, darling," she begged. "Please get well."

One evening, she arrived unexpectedly. Normally, visitors weren't allowed at night, but Mum had a way of getting around rules. She held my hand and said, "Darling, if you'll just get better, I'll take you anywhere you want to go . . . anywhere in the world! Where would you like to go?"

"Fer . . . lady," I mumbled.

"What, darling?"

I knew the songs of *My Fair Lady* off by heart because Dad played the record all the time in the living room, but I wanted to see it on Broadway. Even though New York City seemed impossibly far away, I had distinctly heard Mum say *anywhere in the world*.

When I was discharged ten days later, Mum arrived with my clothes. "I have a surprise for you," she said. "We're taking the train to New York City!"

Uncle Langbourne's apartment on the Upper East Side of Manhattan shimmered with chandeliers and polished marble floors. Up a spiral staircase, in the guest room Mum and I shared, there were tiny buzzers to ring for breakfast in bed, but I snuck down the back staircase like Eliza Doolittle and spent my time in the kitchen, chatting with the cook. At the theater that night, our seats were so close to the stage that I could see the sweat on the faces of Rex Harrison and Julie Andrews. Professor Higgins treated Eliza exactly the way Dad treated me: "Stop saying *um* before you speak!" "The word isn't *kids*, it's *children*!" "Don't slouch!" and "Pick up your feet when you walk!" I knew exactly how Eliza felt, but somehow the instructions sounded happier when they were sung to music.

EVERY SUMMER, WE MADE a lengthy pilgrimage to visit our cousins in Virginia. Seven of us were crammed into Dad's red Pontiac station wagon, our luggage strapped to the roof rack. It took two days, driving south on Route 15 in humid ninety-degree heat. There was no air conditioning, so all the windows were rolled down wide. Sandy, Robin, Victor and I were squished in the middle row, while Chris lay in the back, hemmed in on all sides by a jumble of toys, overnight bags and our wicker picnic hamper. In the front seat, Dad was coiled up tight around the steering wheel, trying to listen to classical music on the radio. Mum had been nagging him for miles to stop so the boys could pee beside the road, but Dad would stop only for gas.

"Alec! Pull over!" she said, but Dad wouldn't stop. "I said *stop!*" she shouted, but Dad only stepped on the accelerator.

It was embarrassing to be in the same car with a bunch of little brothers clutching their legs, squirming and whimpering, so I hung out the window, trying to act aloof and sophisticated. I was wearing a white, sleeveless blouse and my brand-new Bermuda shorts that Mum let me order from the Sears catalogue, so I just smoothed my ponytail and let the wind cool my neck, pretending to be somewhere else.

"I don't know why you have to be so mean!" Mum said to Dad, as she leaned over and punched in the cigarette lighter. She lit her cigarette and exhaled out the window, her elbow resting on the window ledge and her red fingernails tapping the doorframe. Suddenly, her left hand shot over and twisted the radio knob to a news station. She cranked the volume up high. Dad slapped her hand and switched the dial back to his classical music. Mum glared at Dad. His eyes flickered to me in the rearview mirror.

"Plum!" he shouted. "Who is this composer? Quick!"

I had no idea who the composer was.

"Who. Is. This. Composer?" Dad repeated. "*Answer me!*"

Frantically, I searched the sky, praying for the universe to deliver me an answer. Disappointing Dad seemed to be the only thing I was good at.

Dad turned to Mum. "We give her a perfectly good education, and she can't even name this composer?!"

"Bach," I said quietly. The name just popped into my head.

"Bach?" Dad snorted. "Of course, it's not Bach! Stupid answer!"

Just then the music ended, and the announcer said, "You have been listening to Little Prelude in C Major by Johann Sebastian Bach."

"Good girl!" Mum turned around to smile at me, looking astonished. "See?" she said to Dad. "You owe Plum an apology!"

Dad switched off the radio.

"Apologize to Plum!"

Dad didn't say a word, but I was electrified, as if my skull had split open. Obviously, all the answers to all the questions in the universe were just floating around in the ether and all you needed to do was open your mind and let one pop in! There must be millions of ideas, brilliant ideas, just floating around, looking for an open mind. This was the great secret: People didn't get ideas. Ideas got people! And I needed to be ready.

It wasn't the first time I'd stumbled on one of the great secrets. Five years earlier in grade 1, I'd discovered the "blue moon" trick to make myself invisible.

Whenever Mrs. Williamson was about to ask the class a question and walked down the aisle trying to decide who to pick on, I discovered that if I concentrated on the words *blue moon, blue moon, blue moon*, she didn't choose me. Then I discovered it worked at home too. Whenever I played hide-and-seek in the garden with Dad, the same thing happened! He'd be inches from my hiding place. Could probably even hear me breathe. But if I latched onto the words in my mind and focused hard—*blue moon, blue moon, blue moon*—the words seemed to suck me through a black hole into an alternate universe and Dad walked right on by. It meant that the power of my mind could put a fence around me! Block my energy! Make me *invisible*! And most of the time, that's exactly what I wanted.

I now had proof that *anything was possible*, even things not yet imagined—*especially* things not yet imagined—and this knowledge was as transformative as it was mysterious. Ideas were the property of the universe. We were just receivers, if we wanted to be. And I did.

Sleeping Beauty

WHEN I WAS TWELVE years old, I entered the local high school. I was terrified. The high school girls wore circle skirts and cinch belts with bobby socks and saddle shoes, their hair elaborately teased and sprayed into beehives. Bad boys trailed after them, wearing leather bomber jackets, pointy shoes and white socks, their oiled hair slicked back in a duck-tail or pulled forward into a jelly roll. They were always pulling combs out of their back pockets and smoothing the sides of their heads. I'd never seen boys dressed like that: Dad always wore a shirt and tie, and so did my brothers. There was a new lingo to learn—"Cool it, fink, stop bugging me!" "Don't have a cow!" "Don't flip your lid!"—and new top hits, music I'd never heard before on any of Dad's records.

I'd worn a uniform to school every day of my life, but now I needed to think about what clothes *said*. Mum didn't help. She bought my clothes at the Nearly New Shop, which didn't exactly sell the latest fashions. It was hidden down an alleyway off the main street, as if there was something shameful about shopping there. The only time she bought me a brand-new sweater was when we were invited to meet Marilyn Bell after she became the first person to swim across Lake Ontario. Now I learned that "good girls" wore their blouses buttoned all the way up, with a circular virginity pin at the throat. Kitten cardigans were the in thing, but you had to wear them backwards with the buttons down the back.

When I tried to save up my babysitting money for a Kitten sweater, Mum scoffed. "Why would you want to be a lemming? If everyone wanted to jump off a cliff, would you blindly follow?" I'd seen the film *White Wilderness*. I didn't want to share the fate of the lemmings, but I didn't see what they had to do with clothes.

That October, my best friend, Andy, who was like a brother to me, invited me to my first dance at the Oakville Club. I begged Mum for a new dress, but her answer was the same as usual: "Why don't you *make* it?" Mum didn't know how to sew, but she'd given me lots of practice; whenever our urine-stained bedsheets rotted in the middle, she'd rip them in half, pin the outside edges together and park me on the verandah with the treadle sewing machine. Sheets got a second life, and so did she. From my perch on the verandah, I could sew and babysit at the same time, while she went to play tennis. Earlier that summer, she'd enrolled me in Singer sewing lessons at a fabric store two miles away. I rode my bike there and back every day for a month, learning how to cut patterns, insert metal zippers and make fabric-covered buttons.

In August, she bought me three yards of orange wool gabardine and a dress pattern that said "Quick & Easy" on the corner. She also sent away for a mail-order dressmaker's dummy. Much to our surprise, it arrived in a shoe box. Despite the elaborate picture on the lid, the only thing inside was a roll of gauze and a bag of powder. Following the instructions, I stripped to my underwear. Mum mixed the powdered plaster with water, soaked the roll of gauze and wound it round and round me until I resembled a hospital patient who'd been in a terrible car wreck. I had to stand still for an hour while it dried. When Mum cut me out, the plaster cast stood crookedly in my exact form— slouched posture and all—and she couldn't stop laughing.

I produced a dress that was pure 1950s: a "wiggle dress" with long sleeves, a high neck and a tight skirt. When it was finished, I put it on to show her, worried I looked like a pumpkin. Strange female curves had begun to alter my tall, lanky appearance. I stood in front of the long mirror in my bedroom while Mum knelt on the floor helping to turn up the hem. She had straight pins between her lips.

"Know what?" I said, feeling shy, but looking at my new shape with growing pride.

"Hmm?"

"Andy says I have pretty legs."

Mum looked up and laughed so hard she spit out the pins. "Don't let it go to your head," she said. "Everything's relative, you know!"

At the end of grade 9, I failed art. Mum and Dad were flabbergasted. I'd always excelled at art. When I shyly explained that a sixteen-year-old boy in my class had demanded my final project to hand in as his, and that naturally I'd given it to him, they decided I was too young and naive for the public high school. I needed to be protected from boys, preferably in a place with high stone walls. They packed me off to an all-girls boarding school in Toronto, asking that I be held back a year, so I'd be with girls my own age. I wept and pleaded with Mum and Dad not to send me away, but their decision was made.

The day before I left, I say goodbye to Andy at the end of the pier. We sat down on the concrete steps, leaning our backs against the wall of the old wooden lighthouse, and looked out over the lake, holding hands. We'd never even kissed.

"Let's meet back here in twenty years," said Andy. "If we're not married yet, we can marry each other, okay?"

"Okay." Twenty years seemed a lifetime away, but there was something calming about knowing this one major decision was made.

If high school had puzzled me, boarding school felt like a prison sentence. Why was I being punished? For Dad, sending children away to boarding school was a regular British habit. In his mind, we were still living abroad in one of the "colonies." I don't know why Mum acquiesced. She once told me that when we lived in Hong Kong, she'd seen children arriving home by ship from boarding schools in England with name tags around their necks—otherwise, their parents couldn't identify them. At least I hadn't been sent to England, but Toronto seemed just as far. I felt abandoned and homesick.

Gone were my carefree days along the lakefront and my creative spaces in the basement. Now, everything was regimented. Behind the stone walls, loud buzzers rang every forty minutes throughout the day. Instead of blue uniforms, we wore green ones. I wasn't housed in the dormitory wing with girls my own age as my parents had hoped. Because we applied late, the only space available was a bedroom up in "the tower," a mostly unsupervised area with older, more sophisticated girls. Whenever they snuck out onto the roof at night to smoke and meet boys, they used me as a lookout.

I spent most of my after-school hours hiding in bathroom stalls reading books, hiding from organized sports, hiding from teachers and hiding from social events. Classes moved at a snail's pace, mainly because I'd taken them all before. To stifle my boredom, I retreated into my imagination. I thought if I slipped a piece of drawing paper inside a textbook and held it at a certain angle while pretending to pay attention, I could sketch out my inventions. This worked well until the day in grade 10 when our formidable geography teacher, Miss Prestwich, marched down the aisle to my seat, ripped the atlas from my hands and shook it. Out fluttered my invention for a handheld sewing machine. Instead of suggesting that I go into engineering or helping me apply for a patent, she crumpled it up and threw it in the trash. She could have been my mentor, but instead she became my nemesis. Until one night, I had a dream.

The dream was so vivid, I've never forgotten it. In the dream, I was the young child of a wealthy industrialist in the late 1800s. My mother had died, so my father hired Miss Prestwich as my governess. She accompanied us on a transatlantic voyage to Europe (Miss Prestwich and I shared a cabin), and once the ship docked at Le Havre, we took trains to all the major European cities. While Father worked, Miss Prestwich showed me the sights. By the time I woke up, I'd grown to love her. Back in school, I behaved differently towards her. I took a renewed interest in geography; after all, she'd personally guided me through all the cities she was pointing to on her maps, and suddenly, I wasn't so bored. What it taught me at the time was that dreams were useful: They could change reality and expand time. Sometimes, my dreams felt more real than my waking hours.

In grade 10, I fell in love with Harry Belafonte. Everyone else was fixated on Elvis Presley, but I was captivated by the rhythm of "Man Smart (Woman Smarter)." I loved the way Belafonte shouted "Smah-*ta*!"

In 1962, Belafonte came to Toronto. I couldn't afford to attend the concert at the glamorous, newly built O'Keefe Centre, but I'd read that he was staying at the Royal York Hotel and was convinced I could meet him in person if I just knocked on enough doors. Persuading a classmate to come with me, we snuck out of school one afternoon still dressed in our uniforms and made our way to the hotel and up the elevators to the VIP floor. Starting at one end of a long corridor, I began knocking on doors asking, "Is Harry Belafonte here, please?"

After two more corridors and dozens of doors, just as I was about to give up, a tall man opened the door. "Is Harry Belafonte here, please?" He smiled but shook his head. Just then, a deeper voice inside the room said, "It's okay," and Harry came up behind him. I was dumbstruck. I didn't ask for his autograph. I just stared in awe at his beautiful teeth. He smiled patiently, said a few words that I no longer remember and then his manager gently closed the door. But my mind was clanging with possibilities: It was true! Life was theater and you could write your own script. Mum was right! All it took was a little imagination!

Gradually, I came out of my shell. At school, I joined the extracurricular drama club run by the actress Clare Coulter, an alumna who'd come back to direct *Toad of Toad Hall*, a play based on *The Wind in the Willows*. Although our school prided itself on its academic curriculum, it produced a surprising number of professional actresses, including Clare Coulter, Kate Reid and my schoolmate Margot

Kidder, who went on to play Lois Lane in four Superman movies. During the day, I still didn't know who I was or what I wanted to be. But at the end of the day, I could pretend to be somebody else.

That summer, Tanya Moiseiwitsch, the Stratford Festival costume designer, heard about my interest in theater from her friend at the Oakville Library, where my play *Stone Soup* had been produced five years earlier, and invited me to be a summer intern in their props department. Mum tried to encourage me. She drove me to Stratford, a small town about two hours west of Oakville, to have a look and suggested I could board with a friend of hers. Luminaries such as Christopher Plummer and William Hutt were wandering the backstage halls, but the sight of men in tights, practicing their fencing on the lawns outside, intimidated me. As much as I wanted to build props, I didn't yet have the courage or the confidence to leap into such a sophisticated world.

IN JUNE 1964, WE ALL gathered in the great hall for our formal high school graduation and prize-giving. Our teachers were seated up front on stage in their academic robes, and our parents filled the chairs as we filed in wearing our white dresses. My dress was a disaster. I'd gained so much weight that I couldn't do up the zipper, so my roommate had helped me secure it with safety pins and I'd worn a sweater to hide the effect. I knew it didn't matter. I'd never be called on stage. In all my four years of suffering, I'd never won a prize and didn't expect one that year, either. I kept scrunching up my legs as classmate after classmate squeezed past me to accept their prizes. But suddenly, at the very end, they called my name. I'd won the art prize. I knew what Dad thought of art—nothing but a frivolous hobby—and I was mortified. Why couldn't I have won the Latin prize, like my brother Sandy had at his school, or the history prize, like my brother Robin? It was as if I'd won the booby prize, worse than winning nothing at all. Now, I had to walk up to the stage in front of everybody, held together by safety pins, and embarrass Dad—the person I wanted to impress the most.

The previous September, when everyone was applying to universities, Dad had sat me down at the kitchen table to discuss my future. When I suggested theater or art school, he scoffed and divided a piece of paper into two columns. Down one side he listed all my shortcomings, down the other a much shorter list of my strengths, and concluded there were only three suitable careers for me: nurse (because I was caring), secretary (because I could write) and teacher (because I was good with children). Since I'd spent most of my life babysitting, Dad circled teaching as the most sensible career. Mum agreed, although she expected a husband would soon support me. In her mind, a university degree was a kind of emergency option, much like learning to drive stick shift in case I was unable to find a reliable car with automatic transmission. Raising children was a woman's most important career. When she heard of Wheelock College in Boston, Massachusetts, which offered a four-year BSc degree in Education, she decided it was perfect.

Looking back now, I'm astonished at my lack of participation in my own future. I simply allowed myself to be swept along. I'd been trained to be obedient, so I did what I was told and waited patiently for my future to reveal itself. The trouble with passivity is that it doesn't last. Perhaps if I had been rebellious as a teenager, I wouldn't have felt the need to rebel in my thirties when so many other lives were affected by my actions.

Time to Wake Up

☒

IN 1964, THE YEAR I left for Boston, world affairs were heating up, especially south of the border. It had only been two years since the Cuban Missile Crisis brought the world to the brink of nuclear war, and we were still reeling in shock from President Kennedy's assassination the previous winter. Now everyone feared an escalation of the war in Vietnam. American draft dodgers were fleeing to Canada. The American Civil Rights Act had recently been signed into law and race riots and demonstrations were breaking out in almost every major city.

The events galvanized Mum. She immediately turned her attention to the activities of our next-door neighbor, the nuclear physicist Dr. Norman Alcock. During World War II, Norm had worked for the war effort, helping to develop radar technology, and later worked at the Chalk River nuclear facility, but now he had the radical idea of establishing a think tank that would focus its research on how to achieve peace in the world. It would be the first of its kind.

"He's right!" said Mum. "If we spent as much money on peace as we do on war, we might get *peace!*" Enthusiastic as always, Mum offered to help Norm and his wife raise money. She began swiping things from our house to donate to his fundraising auctions. Suddenly, limos were pulling up on our street, carrying important new board members like Brock Chisholm and a young Pierre Trudeau, all gathering around Norm's kitchen table to discuss his fledgling Canadian Peace Research Institute.

Meanwhile, I tuned out. I'd resigned myself to Mum and Dad's choice of career for me and fallen into a sluggish kind of sleep. Like all my years of schooling before, it was as though I was fulfilling some kind of duty, treading water for another four years before my real life could begin. In September, Mum drove me to Wheelock in Boston, where I enrolled with little enthusiasm. She deposited me in residence, another all-girls environment in an old ivy-covered mansion on a quiet, leafy street where an elderly chaperone stood guard from her bedroom on the ground floor.

Returning home from college that first Christmas, I discovered Mum had donated all my theater costumes to one of Dr. Alcock's auctions—all the exquisite couturier dresses given to me by Uncle Langbourne after Aunt Elizabeth died. When I learned that the highest bidder had paid only thirty-five dollars and planned to cut them up for the lace, I burst into tears. Mum was shocked by my reaction.

"Wake up!" she shouted. "Don't you know the world is in crisis? How can you be so selfish as to weep over dresses when the whole world might blow up at any minute?!" She waved a pamphlet in my face, published by the township of Etobicoke, titled "How to Survive an Atomic Attack." It instructed schoolchildren to hide under their desks in the event of a blast. Andy's parents had begun to dig a bomb shelter in their backyard, stocking it with flashlights and tins of food. I could see Mum's point. None of my dresses would matter if we were all underground eating canned soup. Still, I resented my sacrifice. There was a principle involved: She'd jettisoned my costumes without my permission. I decided the only way to keep Mum at bay was to find an alternate donor, so I kept my eyes peeled when I returned to school.

Soon enough, I phoned Mum from Boston. I'd just read in *Time* magazine about the wealthy heir to the A&P grocery fortune, a fifty-five-year-old man named Huntington Hartford II. Buried in the article was the juicy tidbit that he had PEACE etched on all his drinking glasses.

"Oh, do write to him!" said Mum. "Tell him about Norm! Ask him to donate!"

"Why me?" I'd forgotten how Mum liked to delegate.

"Don't you care about the world you're living in? This

is important!" Frankly, I was still more interested in what was playing on Broadway, but she repeated what she'd been saying for years: "You must learn to wake up!"

One evening in November 1965, I opened one sleepy eye. That was the night in Boston when all the lights went out. Nobody knew how far the darkness extended. Radios and televisions fizzled out, traffic lights weren't working, restaurants began to shut down and people wandered onto the streets in dazed confusion. The only light still shining was a giant full moon. I ran outside with my roommates and tried to be useful by helping to direct traffic. But once the streets emptied, an eerie silence descended. It was as if God had pulled the plug on all the man-made nonsense: assassinations, wars, even the underground nuclear tests. Rumors swirled. Someone said that a man had set himself on fire in front of the UN headquarters. Another that aliens had landed: A UFO had been spotted over Syracuse. Was this the end of the world? Even looters were spooked and didn't go out on their usual sprees.

But the world hadn't come to an end. The next morning, *The New York Times* printed a special issue explaining that a malfunction had brought down the electrical grid for most of the Eastern Seaboard. Still, it was all anyone could talk about. People kept asking, "Where were you during the blackout?" Everyone worried that a more malevolent force could bring down the grid next time, and it occurred to me that maybe Mum was right.

On college letterhead, I finally wrote a letter to Mr. Hartford c/o *Time* magazine, explaining Dr. Alcock's mission as Mum had explained it to me: that the atomic bomb had made war obsolete. In the event of a nuclear war, there would be no winners, the whole of civilization would be obliterated. Instead of investing in weapons, it was time to invest in peace.

Three months passed with no response. Then, one night in early spring, a classmate came running up to my dorm room to tell me there was a person-to-person, long-distance call from someone named "Hunt."

The phone was located downstairs on the main floor, in a broom closet under the stairs. When I picked up the receiver, a deep, gravelly voice thanked me for my charming letter. Hunt said he was sorry for the delay, but he'd waited until he could have my handwriting analyzed. It appeared we were compatible. Shouldn't we get to know each other a little better? I was dumbstruck. Didn't he know how young I was? But I was in over my head. His Southern drawl was contagious, and I soon found myself infected. No matter what I said or how much I tried to steer the conversation back towards nuclear bombs, I couldn't even say goodbye without sounding like a flirtatious Scarlett O'Hara in *Gone With the Wind*.

"Geh-ba-ha," I said.

Naively, I'd expected Huntington Hartford II to simply cut a check to the Canadian Peace Research Institute and mail it to Dr. Alcock's office. Instead, he began calling my residence relentlessly. Word soon spread throughout my dorm, and Hunt's matinee-idol photograph in *Time* magazine was passed from room to room. Whenever he phoned, girls in curlers, hair nets and flannelette nighties flew down the stairs and crowded into the broom closet with me, titillated, while I held out the receiver so they could hear him whisper sweet nothings late into the night, clinking the ice in his PEACE glass.

As much as I wanted to help Mum support Dr. Alcock, I didn't see how my bombed-out phone calls with Hunt could prevent nuclear annihilation. When he gave me his private Plaza 9 phone number and invited me to visit him in New York City, Mum's enthusiasm only escalated. She thought this was a delicious turn of events.

"Oh, how wonderful!" she said. "You must go!"

"But Mum, he wants me to stay with him! Where's One Beekman Place?"

"I'll call Langbourne," she said. "You can stay with him instead!"

But when I arrived in New York, it seemed that Mum had got her wires crossed. Uncle Langbourne wasn't at home. Furthermore, she'd never explained to him the purpose of my trip, and once he found out, he was aghast. Apparently, Hunt's reputation with women was well known. He'd already worked his way through three wives and dozens of starlets, including Lana Turner and Marilyn Monroe. Donation or no donation, Uncle Langbourne forbade me to meet up with Hunt, and I went back to Boston empty-handed.

PEACE may have been etched on the drinking glasses at One Beekman Place, but the Canadian Peace Research Institute never did receive a donation from Huntington Hartford II.

BY SOPHOMORE YEAR, I feared I'd made a terrible wrong turn in my life. My trip to New York City had reminded me of the glitzy world out there—lights, camera, action! Why had I agreed to get a teaching degree? I wanted to quit and do something else. I didn't know what; I just wanted art and theater back in my life. But Dad was unbending. His mantra was "Finish what you start!"

I kept phoning home and weeping, "What's the meaning of life?"

"Pull yourself together!" Dad roared. Then, channeling Viktor Frankl, "The meaning of life is to *give life meaning!*"

Mum was more sympathetic. She'd tasted the glitz of New York in her twenties, working for Macy's and *McCall's* magazine. She wanted art in her life too. Worried about my worsening depression and wanting to inject some hope into my life, she said, "Why don't we go to London in the spring? We could look at the Slade School of Fine Art. Maybe you could transfer!" Mum's old friend Caroline had recently moved to England with her husband and offered us a free place to stay.

On a damp, foggy night in March 1966, we touched down at Gatwick Airport and took a black cab to Caroline's address in Surrey. After traveling for some time, the cabbie pulled up to high, black wrought iron gates. Far in the distance stood a drizzly stone building, the size of an institution.

"This can't be right," said Mum, looking surprised.

We drove through the gates and up the crunching driveway. I noticed the roofline of the building had gargoyles all over the place. Huge wooden doors opened into an echoing marble foyer, and Mum and her friend embraced.

"What a place!" gushed Mum.

"Shhh!" whispered Caroline. "I'm afraid the staff has gone home. My little girls are asleep. Robert's already gone to bed. You'll meet them tomorrow."

We followed her up a winding staircase to a room at the top of the first-floor landing. "I hope you'll be comfortable here," said Caroline, clicking on a small wall sconce. Its tiny light cast dancing shadows up the nearest wall, but the far reaches of the room were pitch-black. Mum and I exchanged glances. Even in this dim, flickering light, we could see the room was cavernous. One bed near the door was magnified by its shadow on the wall, the other so far away that only a dark smudge was visible.

"Why isn't this the master bedroom?" I whispered after Caroline had left. "It's huge!"

But Mum didn't hear me. She had already gone to the far-distant bed, and my soft voice was swallowed by the high ceiling. Jet-lagged, we changed into our nighties and fell into a deep sleep almost immediately.

I don't know how much time had elapsed, but in the middle of the night, I was awakened by what felt like hands crawling over my face. Still half asleep, I tried brushing them away, but the sensation persisted. As I rose through layers of consciousness, I became eerily aware of a presence behind me, leaning over the mahogany headboard. As fingertips slowly navigated the contours of my cheeks, I saw no face, just the edge of a dark cloak in my peripheral vision. His touch was tender and exploratory, as if he knew me and was seeking confirmation, but his long fingers continued to crawl over my nose and lips. Not wanting to seem unkind, I began murmuring my discontent. When this didn't work, I tried to shout.

"Mum!" I croaked. But no sound came out. "MUM! MUM!" I sat bolt upright in the pitch dark, and the hands quickly disappeared.

"Hmm?" Mum's voice changed from a sleepy snuffle to alarm. "What? What's the matter?!"

"Somebody was trying to feel my face!"

I heard silence. Then exasperation. "Oh, go back to sleep! It's probably just a ghost. England's full of them."

The next morning, we went down to breakfast. In the morning light, the house was even grander than it had seemed the night before. Elaborate plaster moldings decorated the ceilings. Statues in niches studded the walls. The kitchen, however, was cozy, with the warm aroma of freshly baked scones. Caroline was in the pantry, handing lunch boxes to her two little daughters, who were dressed in their navy school uniforms, politely waiting to be introduced to us. They led us to the kitchen table, which was already laid with our tea.

"How did you sleep?" Caroline asked, casually, turning back to the sink to wash her hands. "Fine, for a little while," said Mum. "But then Plum had the most remarkable experience! In the middle of the night, a blind mon—"

"Chop, chop, little ones!" interrupted Caroline, whirling around and clapping her hands. "It's off to school with you now." She opened a door to an adjoining room. "Jenny—can you come in, please?" A nanny appeared, whisking the girls away in a flurry of coats and kisses and cold air and door slamming. As soon as they'd gone, Caroline turned back to us. Her expression changed from a smile to a frown.

"Now, what did you say?" She slid onto the kitchen bench opposite us, clutching her cup of tea. As Mum told her what happened, her hand flew to her mouth. "We were warned about this," she said. "The estate agents told us. This used to be a monastery."

"A monastery?" said Mum. "You're kidding!"

Caroline shook her head. "The blind monk hasn't been seen in decades, but your room was said to be haunted." Mum and I exchanged glances. "It's why the house was on the market for so long. Frankly, we don't believe in ghosts, but we decided not to use that bedroom ourselves, just in case." She looked at Mum, wide-eyed. "You're our first guests!"

"How fascinating," said Mum, and repeated the sentence I'd heard over and over during my childhood: "You know, of course, that all ghosts are benign, don't you?"

For Mum, the blind monk became a cocktail party story, but for me, he became much more than that. He was further proof of life after death—and the unseen world of spirits. I began to wish I'd never told Mum. After all, the monk had paid his visit to me. I considered him private and sacred—someone sent from "beyond" to get to know me and guide me. Soon, I found that whenever I was faced with a dilemma, I could go inside my head and ask him a question. He often responded enigmatically, but always wisely.

My first question when I got home was about my career choice. I'd been intrigued by the Slade School of Fine Art, but intimidated by all the long-haired, rebellious students I'd seen there. Besides, I wanted to do more than draw and paint; I wanted to write books and act on stage and design costumes and invent products. Art school seemed as narrow a choice as teachers college. I knew I had a creative imagination, but what did that mean? It was a nebulous calling with no clear path, like being in no-man's-land. In the 1960s, no university offered a degree in "creativity." Now I was more confused than ever. There didn't seem to be any place in the world for someone like me. How could I have the life I wanted?

"Any life can be yours if you make it yours," I heard the monk say.

"How do I make it mine?"

"Change the lens through which you view it."

Changing the lens seemed like such a simple piece of advice, but suddenly, I understood. All the wretched subjects that bored me could look different if I viewed them through the lens of something I loved. History could give me plot ideas for novels; geometry could help me design dress patterns; physics could apply to my inventions. It no longer mattered what degree I was getting; any degree would do!

As soon as I returned to college, I began creating the *PikQuik Papers*, a mimeographed newspaper designed as a study crammer for tests and exams. I published it at the end of each term, condensing salient facts into headline-grabbing stories, complete with photographs, illustrations and satirical ads. By the time I'd put it all together and distributed it to students, I knew the material inside out, and I scored higher than many of the girls who'd stayed up all night with their heads in their books—and I'd had fun! The Blind Monk was right. A creative life was a matter of attitude, a way of looking at the world through a different lens, a novel approach you could apply to anything. And, as luck would have it, the Fates were about to help me with my dreams.

A wealthy Wheelock alumnus had bequeathed funds to build "the best college theater in North America," and the college hired Tom Neumiller, an exciting young director who'd graduated from the Yale School of Drama, to set up the new department. I couldn't believe it. The timing was perfect. Here I thought I was stuck in academia with a narrow focus on education, and now theater had miraculously come to my door. It was as if I was once again peering under my bed and finding Dad's homemade footlights.

Tom had ambitious plans. Auditioning male actors from Harvard, Emerson and MIT to complement Wheelock actresses, he put together a co-ed theater company, which introduced me to classmates with similar interests. We spent hours exercising together, learning how to trust and bond. Each season, Tom chose roles that played to our strengths, and theater began absorbing all my time. A Boston theater critic was giving us good reviews, and in 1966, Tom entered our production of *Jacobowsky and the Colonel* into competition for the Moss Hart Memorial Award. Much to our astonishment, we won. Moss Hart had directed the production of *My Fair Lady* that I'd first seen on Broadway when I was ten, and now his widow, the well-known actress and TV personality Kitty Carlisle, presented the trophy to Tom. It felt like I had come full circle in some kind of way.

The parents of my roommate, Vaughan, lived close by in Cambridge and had taken me under their wing. With five children, their family was just as large as what I was used to, just as boisterous and noisy, but their rambling house was more bohemian, with fewer rules, and I felt right at home. Vaughan's mother was dominant and feisty, much like mine, but unlike my father, who was strict and authoritarian, her father was jovial and laid-back. I loved the story of how, on a lark when they were first married, they'd taken jobs in England as a butler and maid. So, when summer rolled around and Vaughan and I were casting around for summer jobs, I suggested we do the same. The local employment agency was advertising for a cook plus an upstairs maid, and I thought, how hard can it be? It's like auditioning for a play!

In preparation for playing the part of "Cook," I bought *The Joy of Cooking* and memorized recipes as if they were scripts. At the interview, they asked if I knew how to cook boeuf bourguignon and I recited the recipe flawlessly. Vaughan and I were hired on the spot, and we giggled all the way home. We learned that our employer was a landscape architect whose grandfather had been the twentieth president of the United States. She lived in Boston but spent the summers entertaining friends at her cottage in Cape Cod.

In late June, we drove down to Woods Hole in Vaughan's little Volkswagen Beetle and pulled into the wooded driveway of a charming cottage overlooking the sea. Miss Garfield came out to greet us, a tall, lanky, handsome New Englander in her late fifties, looking tanned and windswept. In her arms, she cuddled Mottie, her fluffy white Highland terrier. Instead of taking us up the steps to the front door, she led us around the side to a lower-level tradesman's entrance, where a screen door opened into a large summer kitchen. After showing us our bedrooms in the servants' quarters, she explained that each morning, she would come downstairs to plan the daily menu with me. Mottie required specially prepared breakfasts of soft scrambled eggs. She gave us cleaning instructions, car keys and the charge account to the local grocer and showed us how to operate the hand-cranked dumbwaiter, a tiny elevator in the wall of the kitchen that would send my cooked meals upstairs to the formal dining room. One of Vaughan's jobs as the upstairs maid was to remove the food and serve it to guests.

Miss Garfield was the first truly independent single woman I'd seen up close, and I was mesmerized by her lifestyle: her ability to work as she pleased in the city and escape to her own oasis of happiness during the summers, entertaining guests with her casual stylishness, not a man in sight. She exuded a natural but quiet authority, and with her mischievous sense of humor, she often ended each sentence with a deep-throated chuckle.

Her neighbor farther down the beach had hired a young medical student named Mike as a chauffeur for the season, and he often stopped by to visit. On our off-hours, the three of us would sit on the sandy beach playing cards or take Miss Garfield's small dinghy out on the waves.

One evening, as I was hurriedly preparing a complicated three-course dinner for guests upstairs, Mike arrived unannounced. Upstairs, Vaughan had already cleared away the soup plates and was waiting for me to send up the turkey. Timing was critical because Miss Garfield had ordered her famous hot chocolate soufflé for dessert. As I was attempting to transfer the turkey to a serving platter, I lost my grip and dropped it. In my hands were two drumsticks—the rest of the bird was splayed out on the floor. We could hear Vaughan urgently ringing the bell on the dumbwaiter, but I couldn't stop laughing.

"Sur-ger-y time!" sang Mike. His eyes swept the counter. "Quick! Where's the gurney?" Grabbing the body from the floor, he rinsed it off, patted it dry, shoved the legs back in and raced it to the elevator. I threw parsley at it. When

Vaughan finished serving, she came down to the kitchen and found us doubled over on the floor.

"What's going on?" she said.

"Did Miss Garfield say anything about the turkey?"

"Well, she chuckled and said, 'My, my, this bird has *very* loose joints.'" Vaughan looked at us suspiciously. "Why?"

Mike smiled and flipped open a beer. But I'd forgotten about the soufflé. Now I raced to the oven and peered in. Miss Garfield's famous soufflé was a flat, soupy mess. It hadn't risen at all. Had I left out the egg whites? We heard Miss Garfield ringing her bell for dessert.

"Oh, no, you don't," said Vaughan, backing away with her hands up. "I'm not taking that mess upstairs. You serve it!"

At the head of the table, Miss Garfield was deep in conversation. I quietly sidled up to her left, extending the dish. "Ah," she said, as she spooned some onto her plate, "hot chocolate pudding, I see?"

"Yes, ma'am."

She smiled at me with a conspiratorial twinkle in her eye, and that's when I knew she was an actress too. She'd joined me onstage for an "improv," and I loved her for that.

At the end of the summer, Vaughan and I loaded up her Volkswagen Beetle and drove back to Boston with the windows wide open, singing along to "I'm a Believer."

Summer of Love

※

FOR THOSE OF US graduating in 1968, the economy was booming: Jobs were plentiful, salaries were rising and housing was affordable. I arrived back in Toronto and didn't have to search very hard for a job—one fell into my lap. The principal of an all-girls boarding school had heard of my four-year degree in education, which was rare at the time, since most high school teachers in Canada had only spent two years at a teachers college, and she begged me to teach some of her high school English classes. Seduced by the generous holidays, which would give me ample free time during the summers, I took the path of least resistance and accepted the position, but my real ambition wasn't to teach; it was to write a novel.

Most of the students were only a few years younger than me, and I was struck by how familiar they seemed. All the characters and personalities from my own school days were represented in the classroom: the shy one, the boisterous one, the studious one, the joker. Physically, they even looked the same, as if the same gene pool persisted. Two, in particular, reminded me of different versions of myself: the quiet one who wrote the best essays but had no confidence and the imaginative one who leapt at the chance to experiment.

To the principal, I must have seemed safely conventional, but I was a dangerous choice to parachute into an Anglican boarding school where girls wore veils into chapel every morning and were judged on the shine of their shoes. Remembering how constricted I'd felt when I went to a similar boarding school myself, I wanted to agitate, to breathe fresh air into the place and rescue my students from boredom. My first subversive plan was to find somewhere to live within walking distance of the school, so boarders could visit me after hours without permission. I pictured "boho" poetry readings, with everyone sitting on cushions in a haze of smoke. (It was the tail end of the sixties, after all.)

I moved into the top floor of a duplex with two roommates. Looming over our flat was Casa Loma, a tourist attraction known as Toronto's fairy tale castle. We could see its turrets and towers from our living room windows, and its ornate stable was at the end of our street. Our nightlife was soon one big party. One of my roommates was dating a British aristocrat, the other an international journalist. Some of my students wanted me to date their older brothers, but by 1969, I was secretly dating the son of a diplomat.

Pierre was ten years older than I was, tall, handsome and debonair. Although he was based in Europe, he worked for a Canadian investment firm and made frequent business trips to Toronto. We'd met by chance at a party, when he sidled over and began describing a book he was reading, *The Lost World of Quintana Roo*. Ever since childhood when I'd watched Amice Calverley transcribe her field drawings from Egyptian tombs, I'd been fascinated by ancient civilizations, and now Pierre was captivating me with the ancient mysteries of the Mayan peninsula.

Two days after our meeting, I returned from work to find the book on my doorstep. Inside was a note, explaining that he was flying back to his home in London but hoped to stay in touch. I knew he had two young sons and was going through a messy divorce, but that didn't deter me. We began corresponding. I saw Pierre every time he came to Toronto on business, and soon, the Canadian airline Wardair hastened our affair: It began offering a half-price youth fare to anyone under the age of twenty-two. I began flying to England on weekends to meet up with him. In London we stayed in his flat, shopping the antique stalls on Portobello Road, dancing at Annabel's nightclub and taking side trips to the continent, where we stayed in fancy hotels. I was also getting to know his family. In Chicago, we stayed with his sister; in Virginia, we stayed with his mother. In between these reunions, we wrote long, romantic love letters to each other on thin, blue airmail paper, describing our innermost feelings and dreams. I lived for Pierre's letters with his tall, loopy scrawl on the outside of his envelopes, rushing home from work every day to see what the mailbox held. In the evenings, infatuated love poems poured onto the pages of my journal.

One weekend, I took my journal to Oakville. As Mum and I were preparing lunch in the kitchen, I showed it to her, searching her face as I watched her scan the first page. *As the sun sets here across the lake, I feel the same urgency watching this daylight melt as I did with you, feeling time tick away from the warmth of your bed . . .*

I suppose I'd hoped for a sisterly reaction, some sort of shared enthusiasm for my sexual awakening, but sex before marriage was a step too far. Mum pursed her lips, closed my journal, washed her hands in the kitchen sink and asked me to carry the casserole into the dining room. She must have been shocked. Dad once told me that even on their honeymoon during the war, he'd propped their marriage license on the mantel of their hotel room so the maids wouldn't think they were living in sin. I'd been trying for years to turn my mother into my sister, but now I gave up. After all, she couldn't know what it was like to grow up without sisters; she'd had three of her own.

One Friday after work, I had the uncanny sense that Pierre was calling my name. I knew he was in New York City on business, staying at his father's apartment, but I had no phone number. Like most diplomats' numbers, his father's was unlisted. In my head, Pierre's cries got louder and more demanding, until finally, unable to quell the insistent feeling that he was in trouble, I followed my instinct and raced to the airport. It was a crazy, impulsive thing to do.

In New York, I took a cab to his father's address and timidly knocked on the door of a man I'd never met. Would he think I was nuts? His father's expression changed from concern to awe when he opened the door. In the background now, I could clearly hear Pierre screaming my name.

"You must be Plum," his father said.

Behind him, Pierre was curled in a fetal position on the living room floor, howling in agony with debilitating back pain. How did I know? The psychic connection between us was undeniable, and it had been that way since the moment we met.

A few months later, he invited me to join him in Geneva, where he had a series of business meetings, and I flew to meet him for a week. He knew I'd been working on a romance novel, and he'd booked a room at the Hotel des Bergues to give me "a room with a view." Before he left for work each morning, we put on fluffy white terry robes, flung open the tall French windows and ordered breakfast on our tiny wrought iron balcony overlooking Lac Léman. Croissants and orange juice arrived on a trolley. Each night before bed, I read him my pages and we laughed and giggled at the romantic nonsense I was inventing.

On our final night at an outdoor restaurant on the shores of the lake, I presented him with my handwritten love poems, which I'd had bound in a small leather volume with his initials embossed on the cover. With tears in his eyes, he said he would treasure them forever. Then he reached into his breast pocket, produced a small box and proposed with a diamond ring. At that very moment, fireworks exploded over the lake, illuminating a fountain that floated in front of the restaurant. I'd never felt so happy. When we parted at the airport the next morning, I watched him waving from the window of the terminal, as my plane began moving down the tarmac. Little did I know that Pierre would hang onto that book of poems for the rest of his life or that many decades later, as he lay dying, he would ask his gracious wife to phone me and hold the receiver to his ear so his last words to me would be "I love you."

I flew home and showed my ring to Mum and Dad. They were not impressed. Mum said Pierre had no right to propose. Even though he was legally separated, she said he was still, technically, a married man!

Despite our psychic connection, our love affair didn't last. Five months later, while Mum was away and I was spending the weekend in Oakville with Dad, Pierre phoned me long distance, choking back tears. He told me his divorce had been finalized and, as he had feared, he'd lost custody of his sons. He said he knew I wanted children, but he could never risk such heartache again. He knew it was a deal-breaker. He didn't want to lose me, but he had to be honest and give me the chance to let him go.

Pierre's call devastated me. I couldn't marry someone who wouldn't give me children. Flinging my arms outstretched across the dining room table, I wept inconsolably like a mad woman. Dad didn't know what to do. He offered me tea, he offered me hankies, and still I wept. As night fell, Dad crept in and closed the curtains. I wept all night. In the morning, Dad crept in and opened the curtains, but I didn't move. The dining room table was awash with tears. I wept all that day, and the day after that, until finally my tears subsided. Pierre was gone. Our dream was over, closed like the book that had started it all.

I went back to work shattered and forlorn, as empty as my mailbox. My heart wasn't in it. Even though I adored my students and tried to encourage them to be more creative, the principal thwarted my efforts at every turn. Whenever I moved chairs into circles, she complained I made too much noise. If I sent students out on the street with tape recorders to record dialogue, I was reprimanded. On prize day, instead of awarding my best students with novels, I wanted to award blank books as inspiration with their names as authors embossed on the covers, but she refused. When word got out that students had been visiting my apartment on Tuesday nights for poetry readings, I was hauled into her office.

Dispirited, I handed in my resignation. My roommates were moving on and I needed to move on too.

AT THE END OF JUNE, I moved into a tiny one-bedroom apartment in one of the newly built high-rises of St. James Town, determined to complete the novel I'd started, now rejigged to be a romance gone wrong, set on the shores of Lac Léman. I sold my car, the plum-colored Austin that Dad had grudgingly bought me when I turned eighteen, and lived off the proceeds, hunkering down for the summer to write. I'd hoped to finish my manuscript before my money ran out, but I hadn't a clue how to structure a novel. All I had to show for it was a pile of jumbled papers. The writing life wasn't so romantic either. I could barely afford rent. I was juggling dinner dates, cadging free meals from boyfriends at least four nights a week and existing on bread the other three nights. The summer came to an end and so did my savings. It was clear that I needed a job immediately, but now that I'd abandoned my teaching career, what else was I qualified to do?

As I perused employment ads, my eyes constantly hovered over "Cleaning Lady Wanted"—a kind of death wish, since it was the last job I'd be any good at—until one morning, right underneath, I saw an ad from Simpsons-Sears: "Copywriters Wanted." I had no idea what a copywriter did, but it had the word *writer* in it, so my heart leapt with hope. I may have been genetically predisposed, since Mum had been a copywriter in New York City before the war, but

I didn't know that then. I didn't find her scrapbooks of ads until after she died.

In 1969, Simpsons-Sears was on a roll. For the first time in history, their sales had surpassed half a billion dollars, and they were churning out more and more catalogues. As a monument to their success, they were erecting a new head office on Jarvis Street, a building with a striking modern design that resembled an upside-down pyramid. Security guards would soon stand inside the vaulted entrance while silvery hi-speed escalators whisked suppliers up to the hushed executive suites. But their catalogues were still being produced a few blocks away on Mutual Street in an old soot-covered distribution building close enough to my apartment that I could walk to work.

When I went for my interview, the latest shiny issue of the Christmas catalogue winked from the shelf at reception. I knew its predecessors intimately because Mum had used them during our childhood as a teaching exercise in delayed gratification. I can still remember the smell of the pages.

Each November, when the catalogue arrived, she'd give it to the five of us with a box of crayons and tell us to circle everything we wanted.

"Everything?"

"Yes!" she'd say. "Anything you want, just circle it!"

So, for the whole month of November, we'd fight over that book until the pages were almost shredded. We'd pour over the toys, read all the descriptions and circle everything, each of us with a different-colored crayon: every aircraft carrier, toy machine gun, Easy-Bake Oven and Howdy Doody doll. Then in early December, she'd say, "Okay . . . now go back and circle the ten things you want the most." And we'd spend the next week reducing our haul, crossing out all but ten. A week later she'd say, "Okay . . . now circle the five best things."

As the clock chimed down to Christmas, we'd be debating at a fever pitch the four best things, the three best things, the two best things, until finally on Christmas Eve, with our stockings hung and Dad's fire raging, our little letters to Santa would blaze up the chimney with the one thing we wanted the most.

I don't remember if we ever got that one thing, but I do remember the process: We'd learned to "kill our darlings."

On Mutual Street, the receptionist led me through a rabbit warren of small cubicles into a vast, noisy room where dozens of copywriters were clacking away on typewriters.

Editors sat around the perimeter behind glassed-in offices, while shirt-sleeved buyers with their ties askew rushed back and forth with overstuffed binders. A secretary gave me a typing test, then ushered me in to meet the manager, a thin, balding man with wire-rimmed glasses.

"Why do you want this job?" he said, examining my CV, which I'd tucked neatly into a black leatherette folder beside my bachelor's degree. His fingers were tapping nervously back and forth across his desk like an agitated pianist.

"Because I'm desperate."

His watery eyes peered down at my CV again. "We can't possibly pay you what you earned as a teacher. You're far too overqualified. If I give you this job, you won't stay."

I promised him I'd stay forever. I promised I'd never ask for a raise. I promised I'd be the best copywriter he'd ever seen.

He shook his head. "I'm sorry."

The next day, I began phoning him. For the next two weeks, I called him every morning with an inventory of my fridge, telling him how many slices of bread I had left before I starved to death. When I got down to my last two slices, he sighed. "Oh, all right. We'll give you a try. But we can only pay sixty-five dollars a week. You can start on Monday."

I wanted to fly through the phone and kiss him. My rent was $144 per month. With two weeks' work, I'd just about cover it.

On Monday, I met my supervisor, a stylish redhead with an Irish accent named Mavis. She showed me to one of the small cubicles created by low, blue partitions in the middle of the room. It held a desk, a chair and a coat tree. She assigned me to "small appliances."

The following morning, an enthusiastic buyer named Ed poked his head above my partition and introduced himself. "Morning, sunshine!" he chirped. "Wanna see your breakfast?" He heaved three binders onto my desk. "Take a look at this!" He opened a box and pulled out an electric alarm clock with a trailing cord. "Ain't she a beaut? It's our bestseller! Where's your plug?" Together we observed the minute hand ticking over. "You know the best thing about it?" he said.

"What?"

"It's silent!"

"How do you wake up, then?" I was visualizing my header: "Silent Alarm Clock."

"No, no. It buzzes!" said Ed. "Just no annoying tick when it's running. It's even got a light!" He patted the top binder. "All you need to know is in here. I'll leave it with you for a few days."

For the rest of the week, I studied the binders. There were detailed descriptions of every part of the clock, including the dimensions of the face, the type of paint, the length of cord, where it was made, how it was tested. There were statistics on how many had been sold in which provinces and who the customers were—their ages, marital status and the kinds of jobs they held. I took copious notes.

The following week, Jim arrived from the art department. He carried a full-page mock-up on oversized bristol board. In vibrant magic markers on a tissue overlay, he'd illustrated a romantic bedroom scene. A blonde woman in a negligee was stretching her arms in bed, smiling towards the alarm clock. Her sleeping husband lying beside her was wearing pin-striped pajamas. In the background, a large window overlooked a flower garden. "Here," Jim said, punching an ink-stained finger towards a large, empty rectangle across the top. "You got lotsa room for copy! We're doing a sixty-point header. Ed wants it to really shout."

For two days, I worked on the text. In flowery prose, I described the pearly plastic casing, the warm glow of the lighted dial, the sense of serenity and trust that ensured a deep and abiding sleep, even the extra-long cord that could be plugged in from anywhere. When I was finally satisfied, Ed came back. He looked sad.

"Sorry, sunshine, everything's changed. We need to add an electric heating pad down here in the corner." He explained that each page had to guarantee a certain amount of revenue. His pitch to his superiors hadn't gone so well. They didn't think sales from his alarm clock could support a whole page.

Jim came back and handed me his revised illustration. Space for my copy had shrunk in half. The blonde was still smiling, but her husband had been replaced by a heating pad. "Could you cut the copy by Monday?"

Out went the silky feel of the casing and the sense of serenity and trust. In its place, I wrote about the heating pad, culled from a new pile of binders that Ed had delivered. But by Monday, there was more bad news. This time, Jim's illustration had the blonde scrunched up near the window, holding the clock to her cheek. The heating pad had shriveled to half its original size, and now there was a pink electric shaver visible on a bathroom vanity in the corner. This went on for weeks, as nervous buyers kept changing their sales forecasts. I understood their jobs were on the line, but so was mine. As they kept adding product, I kept reducing and rewriting copy, twisting and turning and weighing each word on its merits. I consulted my thesaurus, eliminated whole phrases, cut adverbs and adjectives, counted letters and measured the length of each sentence in picas.

When Jim produced his fifth rendition, the blonde had already looked at the clock, shaved her legs, hugged the heating pad and now had a set of electric curlers in her hair. I didn't give a damn how long any of the cords were. My copy had been cut to almost zero. Nothing was left of my darlings. There was nothing to show for my time—not even a plug. When the page finally went to press, there was only space for three words: "Electric Alarm Clock $6.99" . . . and I had to fight to keep "Electric."

It should have been obvious that my stint at Sears was the perfect preparation for a writer's life: I had to beg for the job, it paid very little, and every word counted. But I felt so disillusioned. It seemed that all the copywriters in the department were disheartened writers of one sort or another, cutting up copy to put food on the table. After work, I'd duck into Yorkville dives, hoping to catch a glimpse of Joni Mitchell singing at the Riverboat or listen to a Margaret Atwood poetry reading. I looked longingly at her handwritten poems framed on the walls (as I recall, they were illustrated, too, with doodles around the margins), but I was unable to afford their twenty-five-dollar price tag. I was desperate to write something other than ads. My novel was a mess, but I wondered if I could get a small article published. Human interest stories were what captivated me most, so I cast around for material.

Dr. Alcock's sons in Oakville had recently rescued a sunken yacht from the waters off the Toronto Islands. They'd hauled it back to their own dock to restore it and were working round the clock, using scavenged bits and pieces under improvised floodlights at night. The yacht had a famous history, one that I thought might interest the national newspaper, so I raced out to interview the motley crew of teenagers.

When my piece was finished, I took a deep breath and presented myself to the all-male editorial department of *The Globe and Mail.* I was right, they were interested. An editor flipped through the pages and accepted it right away. "But we can't give you a byline," he said. "It'll say, 'Special to *The Globe and Mail.*'" He offered me fifty dollars. I told him I'd rather have the byline than the money, but he wouldn't budge. "Sorry. Against policy. Fifty bucks or nothing."

A few days later, my story was highlighted with a photograph on the front page. The front page! I hadn't expected it to be given such prominence. Suddenly, after all my excitement, I felt betrayed. If they felt it was worth highlighting, why wouldn't they give me credit? Was it because I was a woman? The male photographer they'd sent to document the yacht's new lease on life was credited, but I felt invisible. I knew that female writers in previous centuries had used male pseudonyms to get published—just look at Mary Ann

Evans as George Eliot—but even women's recipes in Junior League cookbooks were still appearing under their husbands' names, as if men provided reflected glory. Why were we so ready to give up our identities? Once we married and shed our maiden names, it seemed to me that we effectively disappeared; I lost some old schoolmates forever. But despite knowing this and questioning it, I was about to disappear myself.

Cinderella

IN THE FALL OF 1970, after I'd been working at Sears for almost a year, I received a phone call from a stranger. "Pierre asked me to call and send you his love," the man said, explaining that he was Pierre's boss and he'd just returned from a business trip to Europe, where they'd met up on a yacht in the Mediterranean. I couldn't help being impressed—what kind of boss conducts business on a yacht?

"How about meeting me for a drink tonight after work?" he said.

I hesitated. I already had plans. I'd been buying a little red portable typewriter on layaway as a reminder that I was a serious writer, not merely a copywriter, and this was the day I was picking it up. I was excited to get back to my apartment, to once again tackle my unfinished novel. But I was also intrigued. Who was this man? Pierre had never mentioned him to me. And why was he inviting me for a drink? I decided my manuscript could wait.

A few hours later, I was inside Julie's Mansion, a gothic-looking restaurant near the Sears offices, heaving my cute red Corona onto the polished mahogany bar. It was to be my calling card, the way he'd recognize me. "I'll be the only girl carrying a red typewriter!" I'd told him. But now I felt foolish. Scanning the room, I could see no single man in sight. The doleful-looking bartender brought me a glass of water. I swiveled my stool to have a good view of the entrance and waited.

I waited and waited. After about forty minutes, I got up to leave. Suddenly, from a crowded table of raucous businessmen in the far corner, a slim man in a dark suit wearing thick glasses with heavy black frames jumped up and waved energetically.

"Jeez, I'm sorry!" he said, as he came rushing over. "I didn't notice you." He looked frantically at his watch. "And now I'm late for my plane!"

"Plane?"

"I'm going to Calgary for two days," he said. "Why don't you come to the airport with me? We can talk on the way. You can drive my car back!"

I was so dazzled by his familiar tone and decisiveness that I folded myself right into his plans. Outside on the street sat his little white Mercedes convertible. It was the same model I'd seen zip by at university three years earlier, when I'd turned to my roommate and said, "One day I'm going to marry a man with a car like that!" At the time, my roommate had laughed. She knew I had no interest in cars, but it was a prescient exclamation. A fragment of the future had plopped into my head, and now here it was—along with Prince Charming, who I dubbed "PC."

Driving at high speed along the highway, PC whipped in and out of lanes as I struggled to keep my hair from blowing across my face and my little red typewriter balanced on my lap. His car got a lot of admiring looks from other drivers, but it was useless trying to talk. We couldn't hear a thing above the traffic. He screeched to a stop outside Departures, grabbed his garment bag and briefcase from the trunk and threw me the keys. "See you Friday!" he shouted and disappeared inside the terminal.

I was stunned. What should I do with his car in the meantime? Where would I park it? What if it rained? How did the top go up? Who was this man? I didn't even have his phone number. I drove home to St. James Town and parked his car on the street. I kept looking back at it, remembering the prophecy that had struck me in college. Our meeting felt fated, as if his sports car were some kind of twisted clue—a glass slipper, left behind for me to find. Despite knowing almost nothing about him, I'd already started to believe in our story. As soon as I entered my apartment, I phoned my friend Margot who lived a few floors below me.

"Guess what?" I said, "I think I've just met the man I'm going to marry!"

Over the next two months, PC and I saw each other more and more frequently. I learned that he'd been raised in a small village north of Winnipeg. The village school only went to grade 8, but a teacher had urged his mother to move to Winnipeg so he could continue his schooling. In high school, he'd come first in his class, winning a university scholarship to study engineering. Later, he'd worked in isolation for two years on the DEW line north of the Arctic Circle to pay for his MBA at the University of Western Ontario, where he won the gold medal. Clearly, this was a man on a mission, someone who knew exactly what he wanted. I admired his discipline. In many ways, he reminded me of Dad. They'd both lost their fathers early, suffered similar hardships in childhood and made sacrifices to achieve their dreams.

I loved PC's upbeat, optimistic nature. We shared the same sense of humor. It was obvious he was ambitious but, more importantly to me, he was principled: earnest and honest, fair and kind. I was in awe of the distance he'd traveled in life, the lessons he'd learned. I thought he was the most impressive man in the room.

PC began picking me up every day from work. Soon we were discreetly spending nights together, alternating between my tiny apartment in the east end of the city and his apartment in the west. I didn't want Mum to know I was "living in sin," so I purchased from the telephone company what was then known as an "off-premise extension." It meant that when Mum thought I was answering my phone in St. James Town, I was instead answering a second phone hidden under the bed at PC's apartment. The other thing under his bed was *The Power of Positive Thinking*, a book PC regarded as his bible. I added *Jonathan Livingston Seagull* to our library. Both books held similar messages. PC had been reading, "Stamp indelibly on your mind a mental picture of yourself as succeeding." I had been reading, "Begin by knowing you have already arrived."

I hadn't realized that loving someone could be so easy. There were none of the passionate highs and lows I'd experienced with Pierre. There were no fights and very few disagreements. We laughed a lot, and the future seemed to be unfurling naturally before us.

In October, PC invited me to take a holiday with him to Nassau. He offered it as a gift, but I was stubbornly independent and refused to go unless I could pay my own way. The trouble was I had no savings. I approached the HR department at Sears. In those days, they had a policy of withholding an employee's first two weeks' pay until the end of their employment, so I explained my dilemma and politely asked if they could pay it now, since I'd already worked there almost a year and proved my worth. They declined.

"What if I quit, and immediately reapply?" I asked, banking on the fact that they needed me. "Then you'd have to give me my two weeks' pay—right?"

"You wouldn't do that."

"Yes, I would—watch me!"

My boss, Mavis, was eating lunch at her desk when I ran in, waving the check in the air. "Nassau?" she said. "How exciting!" Then she described the trip she and her husband had once taken there. "Just outside the harbor, there's a wee island," she said wiping her mouth. "It's not on any map. Nobody knows about it." She licked her fingers. "It's ever so romantic!"

She grabbed her paper napkin and smoothed it out. "Look, I'll show you how to get there." Taking the pencil from behind her ear, she marked a big red X at the bottom. "Go down here to the harbor and rent a boat." She stabbed at the napkin. "Then go in this direction for about twenty minutes." Her red line squiggled up towards the right-hand corner. "Turn here and go straight until you see it." By now she'd come to the top end of the paper and was stabbing at the wide-open sea of her wooden desk. "It's just out there— in the middle of the ocean!" She handed me the napkin. "It's lovely . . . three perfect palm trees . . . white sandy beach all round . . . nothing on it but a few chickens!"

"Thanks!" I started out the door.

"Oh, but just one more thing? Don't swim there—it's shark infested."

When we arrived in Nassau, I unfolded Mavis's paper napkin. Even though her map showed nothing more than the red X and a squiggly line, I knew exactly how to read it. I could see the island in my mind's eye and could hardly wait for our romantic adventure to begin.

Early the next morning, dressed in bathing suits and flip-flops, PC and I left our hotel and wandered down to the harbor. It was already hot and steamy. I carried a canvas bag with cheese, fruit and bread. PC carried our towels and a thermos of water. There was an array of boats to rent for the day, and we chose a snazzy white one with an inboard motor and a thin mahogany steering wheel reminiscent of PC's sports car. We followed an agile attendant, who scrambled into the boat. Like a magician showing us the empty-cup-and-ball trick, he quickly lifted three seats up and down to reveal two life jackets and an anchor. As soon as he dropped the lids, I couldn't remember which was where. Then he flipped the key to bring the engine to life, gave the steering wheel over to PC and jumped back onto the dock As he untied the line and threw it to us, he shouted, "Remember . . . don't be leavin' the harbor!"

PC and I grinned and waved and roared forth with the spray of salt water in our hair. The sun was high above the horizon, not a cloud in the sky. On either side, the harbor looked broad and calm. We shouted to each other over the noise of the engine and peeled off our shirts, feeling the heat on our shoulder blades. I slathered coconut oil around the tiny straps of my string bikini and did the same for the back of PC's neck.

Taking Mavis's map from my canvas bag, I held the tiny

paper napkin up to the horizon and shouted, "Over there—out that way!" Up ahead, there was nothing but open sea, and the coastline gradually receded behind us. After some time, the choppy waves began getting bigger.

"Are you sure this is right?" shouted PC, squinting into the empty distance.

"Yes! Yes! Mavis said it was about twenty minutes outside the harbor." It was also, as I recalled, beyond the edge of her desk.

"But we've been going much longer than that."

"Don't worry! Be happy!" Meher Baba's famous words hadn't yet been turned into a song.

Eventually, a tiny speck appeared on the horizon. I pointed. "Look! There! That must be it!" As we got closer, it was just as Mavis had described. Three perfect palm trees stood in the promised circle of white sand—our own private resort in the middle of the vast blue sea—although it looked more like a sandbar than an island. "Slow down a little!" I shouted. PC seemed confused. He looked down at the console and pushed a few buttons, but we were still roaring ahead full throttle. "Slow down!" I shouted again.

"I don't know how!"

"Take your foot off the gas pedal . . ."

"There is no gas pedal!"

"What do you mean?" For the first time, I noticed that PC looked alarmed. He was gripping the steering wheel so hard his knuckles were white. We were barreling towards the island at warp speed and the beach loomed larger and larger. "I thought you were an engineer," I shouted. "How can you not know how to slow a boat?"

"I've never driven a boat before!"

I hadn't either. I'd canoed and sailed, but I'd never driven a motorboat in my life. "Steer in a circle then, until we figure it out."

Around and around we went. Eventually, the engine flooded, and it came to a spluttering halt in chest-deep water. I was ecstatic.

PC lifted the seats, looking for the anchor. He pulled out a strange-looking contraption that appeared to be in two parts, one set of hooks jangling loosely above the other. It didn't look like any anchor I'd ever seen, but, with a shrug, he threw it overboard and we waded ashore, carrying our towels and picnic bag high above our heads.

Mavis was right. The island was cut off from the world in the middle of nowhere, the stuff of dreams. A cluster of tall palm fronds stood waving in the middle, surrounded by a wide beach of sugar-white sand. Curiously, a few scrawny chickens pecked at the scrub. We laid out our towels, succumbed to romantic seduction and fell into a deep sleep. Several hours ticked by.

I awoke first. My arm felt the heat of PC's back. I gave him a gentle stroke and lifted my head. The sun had lowered in the west. A few clouds skittered across the sky. I noticed PC's eyeglasses lying on top of our bathing suits where we'd thrown them on the sand. I wondered how we were going to start the engine. I looked over at the boat. It was no longer there.

"PC, wake up! Wake up! The boat's gone!"

"What?" He bolted upright and grabbed for his glasses. We peered into the distance. About a quarter of a mile away, we saw a tiny white dot.

"Oh my God," I screamed, "it's drifted away!" I grabbed my bikini and threw PC his swim trunks. "Quick, we have to swim for it!"

"But didn't Mavis say the waters were shark infested?"

"Yes, but if we don't get it now, we'll die here! Nobody knows we left the harbor, nobody knows where we are!" I noticed PC seemed frozen, looking out at the horizon with his hands shielding his eyes. "Hurry up!" I said. "What's the matter?"

"I don't know how to swim."

"What do you mean?"

"I never learned how!" PC looked at the boat on the horizon and then back at me. "You'll have to go get it."

"What?!" I was incredulous. Adrenaline was coursing through my body. I knew I was a strong swimmer. I knew I could reach the boat, but my mind was making decisions faster than I could think. What would happen after I got there? The sides were too high. I wouldn't be able to get in! And even if I did, how would I know how to start the engine? I also knew that the longer we stood there debating, the farther the boat would drift. I had all my lifesaving badges, so I made the decision. "I'll give you a rescue carry," I said.

"You lie on your back. I'll hold your head above water. I won't let you go."

"What about my glasses?"

"Don't worry about your glasses!"

"But I'm blind without my glasses."

"Blind?"

"Legally blind. I can't lose my glasses!"

How did I not know any of this before? Terror was creeping into his voice. I now understood why his lenses looked like coke bottles. We needed string, and the only string I could think of was on my bikini. Ripping off my top and wrapping it around the back of his head, I tied the ends to the stems of his glasses. Leaving behind our canvas bag and towels for future lovers to wonder about, we waded into the ocean. If we'd had pen and paper, I might have left a goodbye note. Hopefully, we looked scary enough to ward off the sharks: one topless female carrying a four-eyed male with a bra on the back of his head. I wondered what our shape looked like from below.

After I'd been swimming on my side for about five minutes, several shadowy forms began to stalk us from beneath. They looked like flapping, gray blankets. I could feel the swoosh of water against my legs. Terrified they were stingrays, I scissor-kicked frantically, swimming as fast as I could. I learned only later that they were more likely manta rays, whose wide cloaks may have hidden and protected us from sharks. I said nothing to PC, who was lying rigid on his back with his eyes closed, his head held aloft in the crook of my elbow. It's amazing how far—and how fast—you can swim when your life is on the line. It's also amazing how courageous and trusting a nonswimmer can be when he has no other choice.

Getting to the boat was one thing, but boarding it seemed impossible. I was exhausted by then. The boat's slippery side towered above us. To me, it looked like Mount Everest. I was afraid to let go of PC for fear he might drown, yet there seemed no way to climb up. Finally, we found the anchor rope draped over the back. We both grabbed hold of it, and I crouched down so PC could use my spine as a step. Once he was up and over the side, he pulled me up after him, my bikini top still tied to his eyeglasses. Miraculously, the engine roared to life with a turn of the key, and we headed back the way we came.

YOU'D THINK I'D BE WARY of a legally blind nonswimmer who, despite an engineering degree, couldn't figure out how to operate a boat or put together an anchor, and you'd think he'd be wary of a cockeyed romantic who'd persuaded him to join some chickens on a sandbar in the middle of the ocean based on a map scribbled on a cocktail napkin, but a few months later, we decided to marry. Friends threw us parties. Colleagues wished us well. From time to time, I looked down at my engagement ring and wondered if I was doing the right thing, but I shooed those thoughts from my mind as normal pre-wedding jitters. I'd grown up believing that opposites attract.

Mum seemed perplexed that I'd chosen to marry a busi-
nessman, especially one who was more than a decade older
than I was. She'd expected me to marry a starving artist.
But I saw myself as the artist, and I didn't want to starve.
I'd absorbed her practical idea that I needed a provider. It
would be decades before I would see our island trip as a
metaphor for our entire marriage: PC's blindness and his
trust in me, my role as a small step boosting him up over the
side; and my escape from the circling sharks, getting us to
the boat just in time—even if we went back the way we
came in the end.

We married the following June. PC was pleased. Dad
was pleased. It seemed I was finally pleasing everyone,
becoming who others wanted me to be.

After our wedding, we flew to Sardinia and later to the
south of France, driving along the coast of the French
Riviera, through Nice and Cannes and up into the hills to
the small village of Saint-Paul-de-Vence. We booked into
La Colombe d'Or, an enchanting hotel where artists from
the forties and fifties often paid for their meals with original
art. Small framed oils by Picasso, Matisse and Chagall hung
on the plaster walls. At night, I longed to explore the galleries
and cafés that stayed open late in the cobblestone alleyways
outside our hotel, but PC was disciplined in his habits and
insisted on going to bed early.

One night I decided to venture downstairs on my own.
Timidly, I walked into the hotel bar, expecting to find a
crowd of revelers speaking French, but it was almost empty.

There was only one other person standing there, a slight man with close-cropped black hair, an open face and luminous eyes. He saw me come in and smiled broadly as if he'd been expecting me. The gap in his teeth looked vaguely familiar, but I couldn't place him. He was nursing a scotch.

"Hi, there," he said, stubbing out his cigarette in the ashtray. "Name's Jimmy. What would you drink?" His large eyes peered into mine as if he could see into my soul.

Jimmy ordered me wine from the hovering bartender and told me he lived nearby. We ended up talking and laughing for over an hour—the kind of fascinating, far-ranging conversation I craved, even though Jimmy did most of the talking. But it wasn't until Jimmy mentioned writing that I suddenly realized who was standing before me. It had been almost a decade since I'd read *The Fire Next Time*.

When I remembered that I had a husband upstairs, I had to tear myself away. Jimmy kissed my hand. I tiptoed into our room and PC turned over. "Where have you been?" he mumbled.

"I just had drinks with Jimmy Baldwin!" I was so exhilarated I wanted to throw open the windows and dance.

"Who?"

"James Baldwin!"

But he'd already turned over and gone back to sleep.

It was a moonlit night, and I remember leaning out the casement window across from our bed. There was no distant vista. Our room on the second floor faced a shaded inner courtyard. But looking down, I could see a mobile twirling in the breeze like a tantalizing invitation: *Come down! Come down! Come down.* Although I had married a good man, a man I loved, I could still hear the creative life calling me. I yearned to play in the parallel life going on in the bar beneath me, but it was too late now.

CHANGING MY SURNAME REQUIRED mountains of legal paperwork: to my driver's license, passport, bank accounts and department store credit cards, and each time, I felt a pang of loss. Not just a loss of identity, but a loss of independence in some unspecified way.

Everyone told me how lucky I was. I unpacked our wedding presents: gold-rimmed plates, sterling flatware, Waterford crystal, monogrammed linens and a complete set of gourmet cookbooks with my name embossed on the covers. Just as in boarding school when I'd observed how the mothers of classmates dressed, now I studied how the older wives of PC's colleagues behaved. What was expected of me? I quickly learned that my role was to be a diplomatic shadow: to look pretty, be a good hostess and voice no controversial opinions, none of which came naturally to me. Dutifully, I joined PC on many of his business trips and gave weekly dinner parties, making careful notes of which recipes I'd served to what guests on what dates, to avoid repetition. I helped PC choose his business suits and made sure his shirts were neatly pressed and his shoes polished to a high shine. I made friends with his secretary and observed that secretaries seemed to be running the company while their bosses took long liquid lunches, often doing deals on the golf course.

Luckily for me, PC was an outlier. He didn't drink or cavort. He was more focused on maintaining a healthy diet with strict regimens of sleep and exercise, treating his body like a well-oiled machine to withstand the stress and pressures of work.

I'D JUST TURNED TWENTY-SIX when I discovered I was pregnant, and although we hadn't purposefully tried to conceive a baby, we'd assumed it would happen in due course. Overjoyed, I quit smoking and drinking and started reading books on pregnancy and childbirth. Preparing for a large family, we moved out of our apartment and into a house a few blocks north. I didn't love the house, an uninspiring colonial with a dark, cramped foyer, but the area was close to a wooded path where PC could jog each morning, and I soon made friends with our neighbors.

I quit my job at Sears and spent my days hiring painters, hanging wallpaper, choosing rugs and buying furniture. We joined a Lamaze class where we were told that the uterus has no nerve endings, that pain only occurs if muscles contract around it; if I relaxed during the birth, I'd feel no pain. Planning for a natural childbirth and looking forward to the adventure, I concentrated on getting inside the mind of my baby, imagining its journey into the world. The doctor said I was lucky; my wide hips and mild scoliosis had given me a tipped uterus. He called me "a perfect baby machine."

In the hospital room, I dissociated myself from the waves of contractions and put myself up in a corner of the ceiling to watch myself from above. So many women at Lamaze had spoken of doing this that I was surprised not to find them all up on the ceiling with me. The doctor leaned against the door, smiling. "I love watching you in labor," he said. "You're the only woman who looks like she's having a good time."

I expected a quick and pain-free delivery, and it was . . . until the last twenty minutes, when I began clawing at the nurse, begging for anesthetic, wondering what sadist had claimed that a uterus had no nerve endings. But by then, it was too late. Virginia had arrived.

Back in my room, the first thing I wanted was a cigarette. A nurse brought me an ashtray and had one with me. Over the next five days, my window ledge blossomed with vases of flowers and congratulatory cards, while the metal cabinet beside my bed filled with chocolates and bottles of sherry brought by streams of friends who'd come to party. I only saw my baby at mealtimes, when a nurse brought her to me, cleaned dry and wrapped. Until I brought her home, I didn't even know she cried.

Finally, my degree in Education seemed to have a purpose. Everything I'd studied about the development of the brain intrigued me, and everything Virginia did fascinated me. I nursed her on demand, slept when she slept and woke when she woke, never wanting her out of my sight. And every morning, I strapped on pretty high heels to push her Silver Cross pram along our safe, leafy streets.

As PC moved up the ladder, his workload increased and so did his hours. After work, he and his colleagues began meeting at the newly opened Cambridge Club to run endless laps around the rooftop track, releasing so much energy it could have been harnessed to light the whole city. My workload increased too. Eighteen months after Virginia, I gave birth to our son Carter.

We added a playroom to the back of the house, which I outfitted with so much Montessori equipment that it resembled a whacked-out nursery school. Every evening after the children were fed, bathed and put to bed, I changed into glamorous clothes, prepared a gourmet meal, lit the candles in the dining room and, when PC finally arrived home, asked him about his day. He didn't ask about mine. What was there to say? I no longer had time to read books, and my daily account of life with toddlers at home seemed unimportant and trivial compared with his high-stakes deals in global finance. When I played with the children in the garden on the weekends, we could see him working through the sliding glass doors of his home office, but we had to be quiet and couldn't disturb him.

Within fourteen months of Carter's birth, I was pregnant again.

This time, I wanted all the latest fads: to give birth in a tub of warm water, with my husband at my side, while soothing classical music played in the background—none of which were standard practice at the North York General Hospital in 1976. Times were changing, but not fast enough for me.

I decided to be my own midwife, to deliver this baby myself—at home—so I resisted going to the hospital. Finally, at three o'clock in the morning, the doctor was adamant. He began negotiating with me over the phone: "Look," he said, "just get in here! We don't have a tub, we don't have the music, but you can have your husband with you." He sighed. "And I'll let you help deliver." When I finally relented and arrived at the hospital, there was less than an hour to spare. The doctor came into the labor room. He leaned against the doorway, smiling like he always did, arms folded, his white coat hanging open, a stethoscope dangling from his neck.

"Thank God for scoliosis," I said, laughing. "Or at least, that's what you've always told me!" I felt another contraction. "Uh-oh . . . wait a minute." Holding up my hand for silence, I concentrated on the spot on the ceiling above the doorway, taking myself there, out of body. I could see the whole scene from above: the doctor's broad shoulders, the nurse counting seconds, myself in the bed, head down, mouth pursed, panting. PC was at my side for the first time, giving me comfort.

"I think she's ready, Doctor," said the nurse.

"Wheel her in, then," he said. "Let's get this show on the road!"

A blur of hands unlocked the wheels of my bed, and I was back inside myself, rolling down the corridor, watching the square, beige ceiling tiles flash by. As the double doors bumped open into the bright-white lights of the delivery room, I suddenly screamed, a guttural animal howl that exploded without warning. There was a torrent of blood, and I saw the startled, panicked look of an intern off to my right.

"Don't worry," I gasped, feeling the need to reassure him. "That wasn't pain, that was ecstasy!" He looked horrified, but it was the finale: Our baby's head was crowning. I reached down to grasp the slippery head myself, the bargain I'd made with the doctor beforehand, but I suddenly worried my fingernails were too sharp. I'd forgotten to cut them.

"It's a girl!" said the doctor. "You have a beautiful daughter."

"A daughter!" shouted PC, "and healthy!" He laughed with happiness. She looked just like him.

The hospital photographer took a picture and, a few days later, came to my room with proofs to sell. I squinted at the photo. It was a baby, all right, but I wasn't sure it was mine. I suspected they had just one generic photo and peddled it to everyone.

"Why does this picture look identical to the other two I already have at home?"

The photographer shrugged. "Maybe because all your children look alike?"

I was overjoyed to give birth to a second daughter—the sisters I'd always wanted—and I expected to give birth to many more. Six children sounded perfect to me. But shortly after Jessica's birth, I started to cry. I cried in my hospital room late at night. I cried the next day when a bouquet of yellow roses arrived from PC. I cried when I got home. I had already been feeling sleep-deprived and ragged with a three-year-old and a two-year-old clinging to my ankles, but now I found myself unable to make the simplest of decisions, not even which coffee cup to choose from a cupboard of identical cups. I wept at the slightest provocation.

How could I be so unhappy when it seemed obvious I had everything? The doctor pointed out that I'd had three children in less than four years and simply needed more sleep. He explained that people can go nuts without continuous sleep, like in intensive care units when they are woken every two hours to check their vital signs. Postpartum depression wasn't readily diagnosed in those days, and looking back, I now believe mine went undetected.

We sponsored a mother's helper from England, and I began taking the children to Oakville on weekends, where Mum offered to help me cope. Like many mothers, she blamed her son-in-law, who was largely absent. Photographs of that era show me almost anorexic with the weight loss of loneliness. I'd married a faithful man, a generous man, a man I loved, but the traits we'd originally admired in each other—his ambition and discipline; my creativity and originality—were the things we now began to belittle. I complained about his workaholism, while he dismissed my blue-sky thinking as a crazy, impractical waste of time. I mocked his health routines. Nothing, not even the needs of his children, could interrupt his meditation twice a day or his early morning jogs. He took enormous financial risks without consulting me, claiming this was so I wouldn't worry, but I felt insulted and shut out, no longer part of his team.

Instead, I found myself facing away, forming a team with the children. I poured my creative energy into domestic pursuits: baking elaborate cakes, making the children's clothes, putting on puppet shows and building doll houses, but it wasn't enough.

I trusted PC to be faithful, but his work fueled my jealousy and resentment more than any mistress could. The phone beside our bed often rang at three in the morning when the overseas markets opened. If I grabbed it first and shouted, "How dare you call at this hour!" PC would explode in fury. I continued to give endless dinner parties for his business associates and their wives, but I felt myself drifting further and further away. I couldn't relate to the superficial cocktail chatter. I was certain I wasn't alone. In private conversations, I learned that other women I knew were struggling for identity. We'd been caught in the changing currents: swept into stagnant pools at home as wives and mothers just as the second wave of feminism was encouraging us to swim towards open water. Who or what were we trying to be? *Housewife* had become a dirty word, but so was the word *feminist*.

One morning, a government census-taker knocked on our door, his eyebrows cocked into question marks as his pen prepared to tick a box under Profession.

"Housewife, I presume?" he said.

"No," I said firmly. "*Mother.*"

"I'll have to write that in!" he said, grinning. "Nobody's ever given me that answer before." *Mother,* I thought angrily,

*the most important job in the world and it's not even on the government's
list of professions!* I refused to self-identify as a housewife, as
if we were chattel, as if there was no better descriptor for
our identity than the type of building we lived in. According
to the banks, we were no longer even responsible, independent adults; in 1976, a married woman couldn't get a loan
without her husband's signature.

PC gave me a monthly "household allowance" and
never denied me if I asked for extra, but having to ask felt
demeaning. Marketing men must have figured this out,
because grocery stores soon began carrying cosmetics, jew-
elry and clothing, so wives could sneak incidentals onto
their food bills without asking. Perhaps it was all in my
head, but it seemed to me that husbands in our comfortable,
upper-middle-class neighborhood were growing fatter and
happier, while their wives looked thinner and sadder; I
knew some were on antidepressants. Did every generation
need some kind of opiate to get through life, some kind of
twilight sedative to take the edge off reality? My mother's
poison was her evening cocktail, and mine was a cigarette,
but I was shocked one afternoon in the late seventies when
I joined a mothers' tea party and was offered cocaine in a
specially designated sugar bowl. That was one slippery slope
I refused to go down.

MY LITTLE RED TYPEWRITER, collecting dust in a cupboard,
was a constant reminder of the dreams I once had. The
cupboard was where I stored my art and sewing supplies.

While the children napped in the afternoons, I started PlumLoco, a small company whose name reflected my mental health. I wrote children's stories, invented products, sewed hundreds of gingham sunhats to sell to children's boutiques and designed stationery, which I sold to a local shop. One of my illustrated birth announcements showed a surprised goose laying a golden egg, but it was only wishful thinking. When I took my innovative pram design to a manufacturer, explaining how it transformed with a click of a button from a baby carrier to a car seat to a stroller, he waved me away as an irritant, and when I reimagined a whole car where infant car seats came standard and folded up and down like armrests, he told me Detroit wasn't interested in retooling for the parent market. None of my business ideas made any money, but they gave me an identity, something other than "housewife," and I clung to the value of that.

Mum suggested I stop trying to invent things and get one of my children's stories published. *Down in the Dumps* was a book-length limerick I'd written with an environmental message about a garbage collector. I'd been enraged by the new city rule that all garbage had to be sealed in green plastic bags. Until then, we'd simply tossed our loose garbage into metal cans. Suddenly, plastic bags were everywhere, and I was furious. Why were we being forced to buy plastic bags that went immediately into a landfill? I sent my illustrated manuscript off to a publisher, but a rejection letter arrived in the mailbox. I showed it to Mum.

"Don't worry," she said, "it just shows that most people . . ."

"Have no imagination?"

"Yes!" She laughed.

Tipping Point

TO AN OUTSIDER, our marriage may have looked like a peaceful landscape, but the pressure was building. Small fissures were forming. I'd stopped wearing my wedding ring, but nobody noticed. I'd often complained that my husband was absent, but perhaps it was time to admit that the one who was absent was me. By 1978, I knew I'd lost all sense of myself. It seemed my entire identity had been reduced to a cupboard, and I couldn't shake the feeling that I was a sellout—an artist who'd defected to suburbia.

Desperately wanting to pull myself together, I rented a studio where I could go two mornings a week to write and paint. I took my notebooks, blank canvases, brushes

and paints and my little red typewriter. I also took my tape
deck, but I played only one song over and over: Marianne
Faithfull's "The Ballad of Lucy Jordan." It had become my
theme song. I longed to feel the freedom of wind in my hair.
One morning, as I sat at the wooden table in my studio, with
its windows overlooking a park, an eerie feeling descended.
I'd just opened my journal, poised to write, when I sensed
the presence of the Blind Monk. Suddenly, my pen seemed
to flow rapidly of its own volition. The handwriting didn't
even look like mine. It was loopy and jumbled, but the title
was clear: "The Gift-Jar Is Me."

Into a cave, she went. She dressed herself in coarse
white robes and asked that she be brought the largest
and heaviest gift-jar they could find. "It must be so
large and so heavy," she said, "that I can barely move
it but a few inches at a time. It must be so large and
so heavy that as I grow older and weaker, I will soon
be unable to move it at all." And into this gift-jar
she put all her love and hopes for the man, all the
treasures of her soul. As they floated up in a vapor
and tried to escape from the mouth of the jar, she
weighted them down with kisses and stuffed in blankets of sweat after that. "There!" she said. "I have
protected myself from me. However strongly I wish
to give of myself to this man, I know I must carry the
gift-jar before me, for the gift-jar is me, and it is too
heavy to give. Its sheer weight will remind me of the

energy required and I will grow increasingly too weak to deliver it."

When I read it, I didn't know what it meant. Was it a prayer or a parable?

Hauling out my paints, I began attacking a canvas with vengeance. The images that emerged were so dark and bleak, they scared me. One large canvas showed a naked woman in an empty bathtub giving birth to a bloody fetus as a doctor sat impassively on the side of the tub with a stethoscope around his neck. The painting was ambiguous. Was it a miscarriage or an abortion scene? I was shocked. The woman's face was obscured—was it me?

I confessed none of these things when I returned home at noon. I greeted the children with outstretched arms. But I felt like I was splintering into two people: One was the real me and the other was a shadow self, a character in a play, a character who knew how to get good reviews, but I hated playing her.

I'd always cradled the romantic idea of marriage—an intimate partnership, lively discussions, shared interests and common goals. Instead, I found myself largely alone. When I'd met PC, he was thirty-six and I was twenty-four. I knew that he'd grown up under straitened circumstances and I admired his ambition to become financially independent, but I didn't appreciate how time-consuming his goal would be, or the sacrifices required. Growing up, he'd had none of the material security I'd had, yet I expected him to know that what his family needed most was his presence. I hated sacrificing family time for the fancy things we were surrounding ourselves with. In my mind, we had more than enough. As the gradual loss of intimacy hardened my heart, PC felt my disdain but didn't understand its danger or what it might portend. I didn't either.

In many ways, the trajectory of our marriage seemed to mirror that of the city. We'd lived through a boom in the early 1970s, but over the next ten years, inflation rose to over eleven percent, mortgage rates hit an all-time high, divorce rates skyrocketed and everything seemed poised for a crash. There were major job losses and a spike in crime— especially assaults against women. And then one night in 1978, it happened too close to home.

One evening in late spring, our beloved live-in nanny, Christine, went out to meet up with her friends. She'd come from Wales the year before for a kind of gap year and often met up with other young English nannies at a pub downtown. Close to midnight, she caught the bus home. She used a popular shortcut, a wooded path that led to our street. She could see our porch lights through the trees. Still, it was dark, and she was cautious, so as she hurried, she kept glancing back over her shoulder, never expecting a man to suddenly enter the path up ahead and come towards her. Not wanting to make eye contact, she kept her head down. She was only a few yards from home. As he brushed past her, she heard him hiss, "I'm going to get you!"

Before she could react, he'd grabbed her from behind and thrown her to the ground. She screamed and fought, clawing at him with her fingernails.

I was in bed, suddenly awakened by loud shouts. Jumping to the window, I saw our neighbor outside in his dressing gown running towards the path, yelling, "What's going on out there?"

I heard voices and sobs. Saw darting figures. A frantic banging on our front door seemed to shake the whole house. PC and I raced downstairs. Our neighbor was carrying Christine in his arms. Her face was covered with a dark, leaking fluid.

"Call the police!" the neighbor shouted. "She's just been attacked!"

I ran to the kitchen and dialed 911. "She's covered in blood!" I screamed into the phone.

"No, no, no," shouted PC from the hallway, "it's not blood—it's mud!"

Police arrived within minutes. Beams from their flashlights bounced off the trees and shrubs. Meanwhile, I covered Christine with a blanket and hugged her tightly in my arms. She was in shock, shivering uncontrollably. Two detectives arrived and began to question her in the dining room. After noting her name and age and other perfunctory details, one of them said, "What were you wearing?"

"This," she said, opening the blanket, showing her torn, long-sleeved red silk blouse and black trousers.

"Was your blouse buttoned up?" he asked.

"What?" said Christine.

"How many buttons were undone? Would you say one? Or maybe more?"

"What are you insinuating?" I said. I was standing behind her chair, outraged by their line of questioning. "What difference should it make what a woman is wearing? Why aren't you asking what *he* wore?"

"We're getting to that, ma'am. We just need to get all the facts."

I stayed with Christine that night. Until then, I'd viewed her as a sister, but that night, she felt more like my daughter. I couldn't imagine sending her upstairs to her bedroom on the third floor, alone and afraid. I held her tightly in my arms, trying to quell her shaking, trying to keep her warm. The trauma had sent her deep within herself, and she continued to tremble uncontrollably, like a fragile leaf in a storm.

Despite Christine's description of her attacker, the police found no one when they combed the area. She had scratched her attacker badly, but the police never took samples from her fingernails or queried neighbors. As far as I know, there was no further investigation. What was a stranger doing, stalking our empty residential street at midnight looking for a random victim? I couldn't help wondering if he lived nearby.

To my great sadness, but unsurprisingly, Christine flew back to her parents in England. How could she ever feel safe in our neighborhood again?

A few years later, less than a mile from our house, another nanny named Christine—Christine Prince—was abducted after coming home late on the streetcar. Her naked body was found the next day, raped, beaten and face down in water, and her murder was never solved. Could her attacker have been the same man?

Over the next few years, there were so many alarming assaults that women began chalking body outlines on sidewalks where women had been attacked. "Take back the night!" was the new rallying cry. But some people continued to insinuate that women were partly to blame. We were asking for it. It served us right.

Why were you taking a bus home so late at night?

How many buttons on your blouse were undone?

THE COUNTRY WAS ON THE brink of depression, and now I was too. PC was traveling for business two-thirds of the year, while I remained behind with our children. There is nothing lonelier than being in a marriage without a partner, and a subversive thought entered my mind: If my husband was never home, what was the point in staying married? Other wives in our social circle must have been coming to the same conclusion, because marriages began failing like badly built bridges. The first wave of shell-shocked men didn't stay single for long, however. At one second-wedding reception, I asked the groom what he loved best about his new bride. (I'd always admired his previous wife, an accomplished, intelligent woman.) He seemed surprised by my question.

Glancing down the lawn to where his new bride stood in her wedding dress, surrounded by admirers, he finally shrugged and said, "She doesn't talk! Christ, the last thing I need when I get home after work is a woman who wants *to talk*."

LIKE SO MANY MAJOR DECISIONS in my life, the decision to leave my marriage was triggered by something small—the tipping point, a final piece of straw. I'd fed and bathed the children, put them to bed, cleaned the kitchen, changed my clothes, cooked a romantic gourmet meal, lit the candles and waited for PC to come home from the office. I waited and waited.

When he finally arrived near midnight, he carried his papers to the table and complained that there was no skim milk, the only kind he would drink. I obediently, and imme-diately, drove to the twenty-four-hour Becker's milk store, a short five minutes away. Sometimes we know in real time that we will remember a specific moment for the rest of our lives. There is a weird hyper-realism about it, as if it's being etched in our brain. I remember walking into Becker's, the bright fluorescent lights, seeing the cooler at the back of the store, knowing that if I walked down the length of the aisle towards it, my life would change forever. There were no other customers, just me. I walked to the back, opened the cooler, reached for the carton of skim milk and said to myself, *I will never buy skim milk again.*

That night, I told PC I wanted a divorce.

"You can't be serious," he said. "You're the only woman I've ever loved."

I looked at him in bewilderment. The disconnect between us seemed insurmountable. I thought of all the lonely evenings in his absence, and my hurt exploded in anger. "If this is the way you treat someone you love," I cried, "then God help you!" Of course, the same thing could have been said about me, but I was too revengeful to see it. I wanted to hurt him, to shake him, to make him acknowledge me and understand me, and, in my fury, I didn't hear *him*. He was offering an open door, but I refused to go through.

We negotiated a separate living arrangement under the same roof.

"Mummy needs a bedroom of her own now," I told our five-year-old son. "Will you move in with the girls, so I can borrow yours?"

But a week later, returning from a business trip, PC came bounding up the stairs to our bedroom, happily calling out, "I'm home!" only to find me in Carter's room, hanging my clothes in the closet and clearing space on the tiny desk for my typewriter. Apparently, he had forgotten all about our separation.

My godmother, Aunt Susanne, a tall, large-boned, God-fearing spinster, flew up from Washington to give me a stern rebuke. "I want y'all to know," she said in her thick Southern drawl, "that if y'all divorce, y'all be the first ones in the history of our family!"

Her message was clear: If I pulled the plug, I'd weaken the family wall. The perfectly crafted image of our upstanding, respectable family, the one we'd offered to the outside world for generations, would get swept away. I began to wonder how many other brides had their fingers in a dike? How many other families were hiding leaks? I don't ask those questions now. I know the answer.

Kramer vs. Kramer was a hit movie that year. Mum gave us tickets and begged us to see it, hoping that once we saw the effects of divorce on children, we'd change our minds. PC and I both wept in the dark movie theater, consumed with guilt and feelings of failure, but it didn't alter our trajectory.

That night, grief-stricken, I padded downstairs to the kitchen after everyone was asleep and poured my soul into a poem called "The Meal." PC entered just as I'd finished. He'd followed the slim trickle of light down the stairs to where it glowed beneath the closed kitchen door. I tried to shield him from my awful words by covering the paper with my forearm, but he yanked it out from under. It was the first time he'd ever looked at a piece of my writing. I watched his eyes widen as he read.

> *We sit here, two Calibans*
> *moodily regarding each other across the harvest table*
> *our round tin plate heaped with bones*
> *we pick at in silence,*
> *he gnawing his, I gnawing mine,*
> *oblivious to the fact that it is redundant,*

like making love to a pregnant wife
the flesh taken at a former meal.
Yet still we gnaw and gnaw and gnaw,
unable to give up, still hungry, our fingers bleeding
indistinguishable from the bones we hold
the fleshless words turned slowly on our tongues
stuck between teeth, sucked in, spat out
searching for something, not finding it.
We put down one dried bone,
pick up another,
disinterested now.
Was it yours? Mine? Can we tell?
All the same with the flesh gone.
Once we hit bone there is nowhere else to go.
The meal is finished
but tomorrow we'll serve it again.

"Jeez," PC said softly. "Is this how you really feel?"

I bowed my head, mute, unable to formulate any coherent words, my feelings hobbled for so long under a mask of decorum. Why had I never been honest? Why is it hardest with those we love? I was afraid the truth would kill him.

We hugged each other then, both weeping.

"I felt your distance," he murmured into my ear, "but I didn't know how to handle it."

We spent the next six months in marriage counseling, driving downtown to early morning appointments in separate cars so PC wouldn't be late for work.

The first question he always asked the therapist in a booming, upbeat voice was, "So! What are our chances— twenty percent . . . fifty percent . . . eighty percent?" He wanted to cut to the chase. He liked executive summaries.

Most times, the therapist just spread his hands and shrugged. But one day he said, "Who knows? It could be one hundred percent!"

"Yeah, well . . ." said PC, "one hundred percent of nothing is nothing."

It seemed we'd left it too late.

LIVING SEPARATE LIVES UNDER the same roof became untenable. I'd hoped PC would move out, so the children wouldn't feel uprooted, but he felt that was outrageous; after all, he wasn't the one asking for a separation. Perhaps I was inadvertently replicating my mother's behavior thirty years earlier when she'd packed up her three children in Hong Kong and left my father behind. Their separation had been temporary; it took Dad a year to admit his workaholism, come to his senses and reunite. In the back of my mind, I hoped we might reconcile too. But our story was different. I began house-hunting.

Several months later, we told the children at dinnertime. PC was so nervous he had cue cards in his lap. He cleared his throat. "Children," he said, reading the first card, "your mother and I have something to tell you."

"I know, I know," interrupted Carter, his mouth full of meatloaf. "You're getting unmarried, right?" Such shorthand from a six-year-old. Why did we think the children didn't know? Children notice everything.

We bundled them into the car and drove them a few blocks south to see the smaller house I'd already chosen to live in. A month later, we divided the furniture, scheduled the moving van and held our garage sale. It was staggering to see all our belongings laid out on tables for strangers to plough through. It certainly wasn't the fairy tale ending I'd expected when we walked down the aisle ten years earlier. I still didn't know what my future held, but I knew we had to get through this.

The place was chaotic as strangers roamed through the yard. We'd stacked the children's toys in the garage behind the house so they wouldn't be part of the sale, but suddenly a man waved a small blue-and-yellow tricycle in the air and handed me fifty cents as he trotted down the driveway. I was wearing an apron with pockets of loose change, and as I dropped the quarters in, I saw Jessica running after him and realized what I'd done. It was too late. The man had gone, and I'd sold her favorite toy. Scooping her up in my arms, I told her I was so sorry.

"It's okay," she sobbed, flinging her arms tightly around my neck and burying her head in my shoulder. But I knew it wasn't okay. It symbolized everything I'd wrenched away from her. And for years afterwards, I searched thrift stores, hoping to find that little blue-and-yellow trike.

The night before our move, PC got word that his mother in Winnipeg had suffered a massive heart attack. I didn't know what to do. My heart told me to cancel the move, to fly to be with him at his mother's bedside, but my mind held my rudder in a steely resolve. Such was my hardened state, my willful disobedience, my determined selfishness to start a new life. I was so focused on my own pain that I didn't stop to accommodate his. Like an erupting volcano, I'd taken out half the countryside and left a wasteland. By the time PC returned, his marriage was over, and his children were gone. He came home to an empty house.

WITHIN A YEAR, we'd worked out our joint custody arrangements: The children would spend every second weekend with PC. By then, he'd moved into a ritzy apartment closer to his office and begun dating other women.

Hoping to explain to the children why they now had to travel between two homes, I wrote them a private story, *Love Is Bigger Than a House*. One Friday night, as PC waited in my living room for the children to come downstairs, I saw him reading the illustrated draft. Tears trickled down his cheek. The children no longer remember the book, so maybe I wrote it for PC and myself instead. It must be stashed in the basement somewhere.

Once our lawyers had finished squabbling over money (and to be fair, there wasn't much squabbling), we were ready to sign. I was to receive half the value of our house, which would allow me to buy a smaller one, and PC was generous with child support. I'd refused permanent alimony on principle (I didn't see why a man should have to support an able-bodied woman for the rest of her life just because he'd once fallen in love), but I accepted PC's offer to support me for three years while I "reeducated" myself for the job market.

Our intention was to separate amicably, but divorce can be a cruel process when you employ lawyers. It's like opposing nations sending proxy gladiators into a coliseum to fight to the death on their behalf. (*Be-half*—now, there's a good, divorced word.) Once you employ gladiators, you've lost control of events. They have their mission—to win at all costs—and all you can do is pay to watch.

Early Monday morning, my lawyer phoned to tell me he would be serving papers on PC the next day. When I asked what "serving papers" meant, he explained that a court bailiff would march into PC's office, thrust the documents into his hands and say, "Consider yourself served." I was horrified. Why such a humiliating public display? Why such harsh words? Why couldn't we meet as well-meaning adults in an office, like we'd done before? Apparently, there was an advantage to being the first side to serve the papers; it had something to do with outsmarting the other side.

Over my lawyer's objections, I phoned PC to alert him. We had a brief but warm conversation in which PC thanked me for letting him know, but unfortunately, he was in the middle of an important meeting and asked if he could call me back. Half an hour later, he called to say he'd suddenly realized he'd be away the next day. "Could you postpone it until Wednesday?" he asked. "Of course," I said. "No problem."

Tuesday night, I was in the kitchen feeding the children when I heard a knock on my front door. I opened it to a tall gentleman who asked my name, thrust a manila envelope into my hands and said, "Consider yourself served!"

A thousand feelings flew through my heart as I looked dumbly at the envelope—incredulity, shock, denial, hurt, betrayal and then anger. This wasn't the action of the man I knew so well. This was the action of a man who'd succumbed to legal advice. We'd been steamrollered by a system determined to turn us into adversaries.

When our decree absolute came before the courts, I tried once again to humanize the events. Since PC's lawyers had managed to serve the divorce papers on me, he was the one who'd been summoned to court for the finale. It felt momentous to me, this final unraveling of our family, and I asked if I could go with him. When his case was called, I stood up with him. The judge seemed surprised. He asked why I was there. I put my arm through PC's and said, "Your Honor, we walked up the aisle together, it's important we exit together, too." The judge looked directly at me. "Is this what you both want?" For a split-second I wondered what he would do if I answered no. PC looked uncomfortable, but he was nodding, so I tried to smile with confidence as I answered yes. Inside, my gut was churning. Had we tried hard enough? I'd caused PC so much pain. I wished I could turn back the clock. But it was too late. It was time to let him go.

We walked out of the building together. I remember it was late fall. Brown leaves and broken twigs were blowing around the sidewalk. At the street corner, we parted ways, PC walking south to his office, and I walking north towards home. A few seconds later, at the same moment, we both looked back—a sad acknowledgment of sorts. Then we turned on our own paths and kept walking in opposite directions.

Freedom

TA-DA! WELCOME TO THE EIGHTIES—a decade of optimism when all a woman needed was big hair, big shoulders and plenty of pouf.

I adored my new house, a skinny, redbrick Victorian with high ceilings and broad steps leading up to the front door. Although the rooms seemed unloved, with dark oak trim and all the walls painted black, I knew I could brighten them with a little white paint. On the front door, I installed a heavy bronze knocker I'd found at an antique market—the head of Neptune, the generator of life, crashing through waves of fresh water—and on the third floor, I appointed a tiny room under the eaves as my writing room. My typewriter faced the backyard, which abutted a property owned by The Royal Conservatory of Music. Initially, our backyard was nothing but dirt. But when I began dating a horticulturalist, he offered to come with his spade and fertilizer and turn my yard into a garden of beauty. Soon I had climbing hydrangeas, honeysuckles and wildflowers amidst sweet-smelling lilacs and flowering shrubs with Latin names that over the years would mature and blossom long after my horticulturalist disappeared. His bridal wreath spirea was a showpiece and eventually cast its veil over half my garden.

All day long, beautiful melodies drifted out over our fence as students next door practiced their violins and pianos. I'd been reading *The Secret Life of Plants*, the bestselling book by Bird and Tomkins, which bolstered my childhood belief that plants were conscious beings who could feel and communicate. I'd heard that classical music enhances the growth of plants, and now there seemed no doubt: The flowers in my garden grew quicker, taller and stronger, and so did I.

Despite being a single mother with three young children, I didn't feel burdened with responsibility; I experienced an exhilarating sense of freedom, the freedom to be me. There was a public elementary school right around the corner, and I quickly enrolled the children. In the evenings after they were in bed, I popped "The Ballad of Lucy Jordan" into our tape deck and danced alone with myself, feeling the freedom as I twirled around, flinging my arms into the air . . . feeling *alive*. It would be another forty years

before my children pointed out that I'd completely misin-
terpreted the lyrics.

Once a week, I hired a babysitter and headed downtown
to Art's Sake, a factory space above a storefront where the
artist Robert Markle held life-drawing classes. His own pro-
vocative murals would soon emblazon Markleangelo's, a
restaurant behind the King Edward Hotel, but I knew nothing then of his notoriety. I was just excited to be around
other artists again. I hadn't taken an art course in years, not
since Virginia was a baby and I'd taken her with me to study
with Gerald Scott. Scott had allowed me to prop her on a
chair beside me, where she watched happily, twirling a paint-
brush, but once I had more babies, it became logistically
impossible and sadly I'd had to withdraw.

I'd never met an art teacher like Markle. He seemed to
ooze resentment   impatient, angry, disdainful. He never
strolled among us offering gentle advice. Instead, he stuffed
himself into an armchair on a raised stage at one end of
the loft like a truck driver crammed into the cab of a tractor
trailer, glaring at us as though we were blocking his way
in rush hour traffic. But he employed luscious models who
were a joy to behold—large-bosomed and curvy, their flesh
dimpled in shadow. They often posed for less than thirty
seconds at a time, continuously moving as if they were slow
dancing. Markle insisted we draw on huge sheets of newsprint with fat shaving brushes dipped in pots of black ink
and demanded we use our whole bodies with wide sweeping

gestures, to give ourselves up to their fluid movements, to feel the curves.

Without leaving his makeshift throne, he brandished a long, wooden stick with a metal spike on the end, the kind garbage pickers use to stab at trash. "What's that shit?" he'd yell, pointing his stick. "Loosen up! Let go! Feel the goddamn thing you see. Breathe it, for fuck's sake!" I'd never heard so many four-letter words splattered so triumphantly into the air.

Succumbing to Markle's browbeating, I was doing lightning-fast work. With a shaving brush, it was impossible to focus on detail; there wasn't time to be careful. Uptight artists soon gave up and dropped out. The rest of us let our brushes bypass our brains, knowing that perfection was no longer an option. At the end of each class, like quivering supplicants, we laid our drawings on the floor. Lumbering down from his platform, Markle slowly circled the room, stabbing his spike into each work, screaming, "What fuckhead did this?" His critiques were crushing. I always trembled with feelings of inadequacy, fearing rejection, bracing for a blow to my ego, but I kept coming back because of the models.

One night, when he got to mine, I heard him exhale.

"Not bad," he grumbled. "Whose is this?" I was standing in the back. Shyly, I raised my hand. He looked momentarily surprised, but he'd already pegged me. "Tight-ass do-gooder!" he snarled. On the way out, he ordered me to chuck my drawings into the garbage bin by the door. "You think your fucking shit is so goddamn precious?"

But I'd hidden the "not bad" one inside my sketchpad and smuggled it home. Every time I looked at it, I remembered Markle's rage. A new understanding informed my thoughts. Rage was important. Pretty paintings have their place—flowers, fruit, landscapes, the kind of soothing, decorative art I'd been producing for years—but great art, art that forces a viewer to truly see, has rage baked in. Robert Markle knew this. Rage gives us something to say. Rage forces the voice out of our throat. So, I taped the newsprint drawing to my bedroom wall and dreamt of being braver. I couldn't go back in time, but this was a new fork in the road. This time, I was determined to give my eight-year-old self another chance, to follow the paths I'd lacked the courage to follow in the past. One day, if I was lucky, I hoped to find my voice.

It didn't take long.

Within weeks, a newspaper ad fed right into my fantasies.

"Extras! Extras! Actors Wanted!"

Grabbing some headshots, I rushed to the casting call, hoping to relive my theater experiences. In childhood, Dad told me my teeth gave me "character," and he'd refused to pay for braces, but now an assistant looked sadly at my photos and told me my teeth were too crooked. Perhaps I'd look okay in a crowd filmed from a distance, or in a non-speaking role, preferably with my mouth shut. They cast me in two films. In one, I was a silent juror in a courtroom drama. In the other, I was a speck on the horizon dressed as a pioneer struggling over a hilltop. The work was mind-numbing. It wasn't what I imagined at all. Most of the time, we sat around on set playing cards. Sometime later, a friend said, "Hey, I saw you in a courtroom on TV last night!" But I never saw it.

One day, the buzz around the card table was that York University was launching a new postgraduate theater program. Aspiring actors, directors, costume designers and playwrights were invited to apply. Playwrights? My ears perked up. This was my chance! Attaching some scripts I'd written in college and a few reviews from my previous acting stints in Boston, I sent in my application. Surprisingly, I made the first cut—but not as a playwright, as one of the actors. Now they required a monologue and a song. They wanted to see me perform.

On the day of the audition, I filed into the auditorium with other hopefuls and noted that I was at least ten years older than everyone else. I was certainly the only divorced mother with children. The student beside me whispered that more than twelve hundred students from across Canada had applied for the twenty-two coveted spots. After delivering my monologue, I nervously awaited my turn to sing. This was the part of the audition I feared would sink me. Singing was not my forte. All through childhood, I'd been the last person picked for any choir, so the only solution was to choose a song I could talk my way through. Wearing a fedora and channeling Marlene Dietrich, I wrapped myself around a lamp post in the middle of the room and threw myself into the lyrics of "Lili Marlene," using my deepest, sexiest, guttural voice. At least they'd know I had guts, even if I couldn't carry a tune.

When the envelope arrived announcing I'd been accepted, I was ecstatic. It had taken me half my life, but I was finally coming home to my childhood basement, my earliest happiness, a universe of invention and creativity where Diana and I had written, directed, produced and acted, sewing costumes, painting props, always making "something out of nothing." Why do we so often forget our earliest happiness? Whatever we did easily in childhood, the things that gave us most pleasure, ought to predict our future direction, but so often, life gets in the way. We bend to expectations or get lured off track.

Throughout my life, I'd had recurring dreams about my basement, which always appeared as a vast system of interconnected playrooms running underground, beneath several city blocks. At one end was a nursery school, in the middle was a huge room filled with costumes and masks, and at the other end was an escape tunnel that exited onto an entirely different street. Of course, I recognized this "base-ment" as my subconscious—a motherlode of possibilities—and whenever I wanted to sleep soundly, I tried to sink deeply into that space.

I was thrilled by what I was learning at York. The codi-rectors of the program, David Smukler and Michelle George, taught us voice and movement, while the mime artist, Dean Gilmour, taught us clown. He helped us search for a character, one who already resided deep within our psyche but whom we'd never met. Mine turned out to be a sexy harlot from the Deep South, always complaining of the heat while sitting atop an air conditioner. She sounded suspiciously like my alter ego who'd answered the calls from Huntington Hartford II in my dorm room all those years ago. I just had to wear a red rubber nose, swing my legs over the edge of the darkened stage and let my character make a fool of herself.

The lesson was to trust ourselves. But the bigger lesson was to trust the audience. Theater is always a pact between the two. It's scary to fly unscripted, to offer yourself up exposed and unprotected to a room full of strangers, but we learned the value of taking that risk. If we were honest and shared our vulnerabilities, the audience reached out to catch us.

AFTER MY DIVORCE, I'D LOST custody of many of the friends from our previous social circle. After all, most of them had been PC's business associates and their loyalty was to him. A few true friends found ways to accommodate us both, but even though I'd moved less than a mile away, it was another orbit entirely. Instead of hobnobbing with captains of industry, I spent time with new friends who were starving artists—actors, playwrights and costume designers, most of whom were single. They weren't constantly checking the stock market or dressing for charity balls, they were waiting on tables to pay their rent.

I became close friends with Jeanette, the only student in our class who was studying to be a costume and set designer, and sometimes I met her late at night at the pub where she was waitressing. She was soon to get married, and I'd offered her my house for her reception. One night, I arrived at the end of her shift to find her in tears, shaking with humiliation. In the busy chaos, she'd served the wrong drinks to a table of businessmen. As they were leaving, one of them had held out a fifty-dollar bill and said, "Want a tip?" It was the most generous tip she'd ever been offered, and she thanked him profusely. But as she reached out to take it, he snatched it back and pointedly ripped it into a dozen tiny pieces. As the pieces fluttered into the ashtray, the men guffawed and stumbled outside, stopping to light their cigars. I was incensed. As I hugged Jeanette tightly and wiped her tears, I wondered how boys turned into men like this, mocking and taunting women with cruel power plays? I had a son. Was it up to mothers? How do we raise sons to be sensitive and compassionate?

I had recently read *Scoring: The Art of Hockey*, Hugh Hood's analysis of Seymour Segal's hockey paintings, and the incident with Jeanette fueled an idea for my end-of-term project at York University. I was to write and perform a one-woman piece. Even though hockey was Canada's national sport, I'd never understood men's love of the sport until I saw Segal's paintings. His frenetic images suggested that hockey was a metaphor for sex. Hood pointed out that not only did the rink have circles resembling breasts, but even the thin red line of the goal was known as "the crease." You can imagine how he described the stick and the puck. Metaphors matter, and when I read the book, a distant memory clattered into place. After once telling a boyfriend that I thought I was pregnant, he said, "You mean, I scored?"

For my end-of-term performance, I costumed myself as a goalie and painted three large backdrops approximating some of Segal's artwork. Wearing a face cage constructed of bras and with sanitary pads strapped onto my legs to mimic kneepads, I hunched in front of the crease with my stick, reciting a kind of staccato poem I'd written, letting my rage fly. Raw, belligerent, accusatory. I raged at society, at paternalism, at the lack of respect for women, at the institution of marriage designed to keep us down, at the delusions of fairy tales—the myths that had promised so much and delivered so little. I wasn't raging at my ex-husband. It wasn't his fault. Men had been deluded by fairy tales too.

From the audience, there was stunned silence . . . then applause.

Suddenly, from the bleachers, a fellow actor leapt from the second row and tackled me to the ground, his version of free-form performance art.

"What the hell was that all about?" I asked Jeanette later.

"I guess you nailed it," she said. "He's a hockey player. I think you turned him on."

CARTER HAD RECENTLY STARTED playing hockey, but I no longer felt like supporting him in this endeavor. Segal's paintings had opened my eyes. The type of jerk who'd power-tripped Jeanette was not the kind of man I wanted to raise. Besides, getting up at the crack of dawn every Saturday morning to cradle a paper cup of stale coffee in a freezing arena was not my idea of fun. I hated sitting on cold cement bleachers, watching six-year-old boys flail around on their ankles, trying to be the first one to get the puck across the crease, listening to their fathers yelling "Kill him! Kill him!" Carter was the goalie, trying to protect his team, but his padded body was being pounded to a pulp by other adrenaline-fueled tykes in a scrum of sticks and blades. Why were we urging our sons to massacre each other?

One morning, as I was removing Carter's skates and massaging his frozen toes, I snarled, "What is it that you like about hockey, anyway?"

I saw his eyes dart towards his coach, who was standing in the wings with a box of Tim Hortons. "The donuts!" he said.

"You mean, I've been waking up at five o'clock every Saturday morning just so you can have *donuts*?!"

He looked up at me with a shamefaced grin.

"So, if I bought you donuts every Saturday, you'd give up hockey?"

"Uh-huh."

I traded in his hockey paraphernalia so fast he hardly had time to salivate. Instead of teaching him to beat up his fellow man in some mad, competitive mating ritual, I enrolled him in swimming. No more icy arenas. No more cold feet. Instead, on Saturday afternoons, I sat behind a steamed-up glass window in front of a warm Olympic-sized pool and watched him swim lengths and win medals—and we stopped for donuts on the way home.

SPRING CAME EARLY THAT YEAR. Over our fence, on the air of violin strings, the climbing purple clematis grew lush and our magnolia bloomed twice, creating a magical umbrella of fragile pink petals to shade the meals we served outside. As a peace offering, the same actor who'd lunged at me during my solo hockey performance offered to build me a deck. He said it was easy, as easy as building a stage set, and he had built plenty of those. Over the next few weekends, fueled with free beer, he hammered and nailed the wood together, while I learned to lay bricks along the path that meandered around the flower beds. Jeanette got married and held her reception there, designing her short ballerina-style wedding dress using yards and yards of white tulle. She looked like a tall, glamorous model from the House of Dior on the arm of her groom, a doppelganger for Clark Kent. I'd never seen her look so happy.

It seemed that everything was falling into place. Mum had always reassured me in my darkest moments that "life can turn on a dime," and it appeared she was right. My life had blossomed. I was doing the things I loved, and within eighteen months, I would earn my master's degree. But a darker expression of Mum's was that "things are never so bad that they can't get worse."

Not long after Jeanette's wedding, I was heading down-town in my little red Honda Civic on a clear, sunny after-noon, listening to classical music on the car radio, mulling over what we'd learned that morning in acting class. We'd been taught how to minimize damage during choreographed falls, to relax instead of resisting.

I stopped at a red light.

Suddenly, from my left, I saw an enormous black Cadillac racing into the intersection. With a high-pitched squeal, it made an abrupt turn towards me, careening around the corner at top speed. As it lost control, I watched it coming as if in slow motion. Instinctively, I relaxed. The Cadillac's headlights shattered my windshield, smashing my Honda backwards into all the cars behind, jamming us together like an accordion. It came to rest on my dashboard. Three men jumped out and raced away towards the railway tracks. Miraculously, I was alive.

I leapt from my car. "How dare you run away!" I screamed down the road. "How dare you!"

A passerby from the sidewalk yanked me to the pave-ment. "Get down!" she shouted. "They've got guns!"

Sirens wailed in the distance. Police cars converged at the intersection. We learned that the Cadillac was stolen. The men had just robbed a bank. Three ambulances arrived. Many people were badly injured, but I felt unscathed. At the hospital, I kept insisting I was fine. I didn't want an X-ray, I just wanted to go home. But the next morning, I couldn't get out of bed. It felt like my spine had collapsed.

For the next few weeks, Mum and Dad took turns coming into the city to help me. I lay in bed, unable to walk or dress myself, much less look after the children. I cried from the pain, the helplessness, the frustration. My spine felt like one of those children's toys where the plastic donuts get stacked on a rod, except someone had removed the rod and the donuts were sliding all over the place. There was nothing holding me together. I was desperate to get back to acting classes, but Mum was adamant: She wouldn't let me get out of bed.

"You need to be a mother to those precious children of yours!" she shouted. "What do you want to remember at the end of your life—a bunch of plays, or watching your children grow up?!"

Perhaps she needed to justify her own life and the choices she'd made, but deep down, I knew she was right. How could I embark on an acting career when I had three young children to raise? I got the feeling she was almost glad I'd been hit by a car. She hoped it might knock some sense into my head.

When it became clear that I couldn't return to university for at least six months, I felt defeated. There would be no way to make up the lost time. I didn't ask for a deferment. I couldn't muster the strength to push my way through. My theater dream was finished. With a heavy heart, I withdrew from the program and moved out to Oakville with the children to spend the summer of 1981 on the lake with Mum and Dad. I needed to recover my health.

1981 was the summer of Lady Diana's "fairy-tale wedding" to Prince Charles, and so, on July 29, Mum and Dad
set their alarm so we could run downstairs at five o'clock
in the morning and snuggle into quilts on the floor of their
television room to watch the live broadcast. Ironically, at
the very time when feminist authors were beginning to
rewrite fairy tales and I was reading Robert Munsch's *The
Paper Bag Princess* to my children, it seemed the world could
still be seduced by the idea of a naive young girl magically
transformed into a beautiful princess by marrying a prince.
Hundreds of millions of people were tuning in just like we
were, hungry for the fantasy.

In eager anticipation, we watched as Diana was paraded
through the streets of London like a fancy dessert on the
tea trolley at Claridge's. Frothed in layers of cream and
topped with a diamond tiara, she stepped out of her gilded
horse-drawn carriage at St. Paul's Cathedral, looking delec-
table enough to make everyone believe in fairy tales again.
When reporters had asked the couple if they were in love,
she said, "Of course!" while Charles famously giggled and
said, "Whatever 'in love' means." But after their honeymoon, when Diana was asked if she'd cooked Prince Charles
a breakfast yet, she lowered her eyes demurely and said, "I
don't eat breakfast." And I remember thinking, *Uh-oh, wait
till Charles is on the menu.* Cynicism clouded the spectacle for
me, because I knew from experience that eventually sleeping
princesses wake up.

Perhaps the wedding reminded me of what could have been, of what I'd lost, or perhaps the car accident had been more traumatic than I realized, but as my physical health improved, my emotional strength weakened. The euphoria of independence I'd felt the previous fall now dissipated into the ruins of my marriage, and I sank into depression. I felt hollowed out, stripped bare, with no props to hang onto—a complete failure. But a failure at what? A failure at playing the role, at following the path that had been laid out for me.

MUM ONCE TOLD ME THAT my first full sentence as a toddler was "I do it *myself!*" I also had a memory that should have been a warning to any future husband in my life.

When I was about six years old, I was sitting on the verandah, playing with my dolls. Mum's friends were sitting in the wicker chairs around me, having a tea party. One of them leaned down and said, "You have so many lovely babies, dear."

"Yes," I said proudly, "when I grow up, I'm going to have ten!"

Chuckling, she said, "I wonder what your husband will have to say about that!"

"Oh, I don't want a husband," I said. "Only babies."

As a child, I'd loved the Disney film *Cinderella*, but I was never one of those girls who dreamt of a wedding. I never identified with the *bride*; I identified with the *birds*. Remember the bluebirds of happiness? They twittered around

Cinderella, fetching ribbons and lace and a tape measure, making her dress from old scraps, chirping, "We can do it! We can do it!" I wanted to be like those birds. I'd also loved Rumpelstiltskin, who knew how to turn straw into gold.

As the summer came to an end and I regained my strength and returned with my children to the city, I was more determined than ever to be like those bluebirds of happiness. I yearned for a bigger creative space—a huge barn perhaps, with every tool imaginable: typewriters, table saws, carpenter's kits, sewing machines, cutting boards, kilns, canvasses, easels. I wanted an unlimited supply of fabrics, inks, paints, putty, clay. I pictured a stage at one end, complete with footlights and an orchestra pit. It would be wonderful to meet a musician, someone who'd play the grand piano while I lay on top in a gold lamé gown, writing lyrics, but mainly I wanted to be original, to do things that had never been done before. I wanted my imagination to soar.

But how to earn a living?

I'd been using PC's three-year reeducation stipend to study at York University, but now that I'd withdrawn without a degree, I had less than two years left to find a job. Nothing focuses the mind faster than being on the edge of a cliff.

I'D ALWAYS KEPT AN "ideas box" in the kitchen. It was a recipe box stuffed to overflowing with index cards for writing down ideas whenever they occurred to me. There were promotional ideas, like Canada Post outlets where you could personalize your postage stamps; goldfish crackers packaged in clear plastic fishbowls; Cadbury's chocolate fingers chopped into snack-sized "fingertips"; superhero dressing gowns for kids; sparkly red Dorothy shoes that granted your wish if you clicked three times—and, of course, my convertible pram. Dozens and dozens of ideas that I'd presented to companies with no success. When they often appeared on the market years later, my children would say, "Look, Mom, there's your idea. You were way ahead of your time!" But I didn't want to be ahead of my time. I needed a project to succeed now. In desperation, I began sifting through the box.

Years earlier, I'd seen the possibility of turning children's running shoes into charm bracelets. Every child owned a pair of running shoes. If I could entice them to collect charms to dangle off their laces, perhaps I could make my fortune. Who better to fuel the fad than McDonald's? They'd recently introduced Happy Meals, and every box came with a free toy. I'd been fascinated with premiums ever since the early fifties when I'd received my first free toy from Quaker Puffed Wheat. Their slogan claimed that their cereal had been "shot from a gun," and I can still remember mailing in the box tops and receiving a tiny ring in the shape of a cannon that shot Puffed Wheat across the table.

With clay and a little paint, I created prototypes of my SHOE-MACs: a hinged hamburger that opened to hold a subway token, a "beefcase" that held secret notes, a tiny statue of Ronald McDonald and a mini french-fry eraser. After dying a bunch of shoelaces bright yellow and drawing rows of arches on them in red marker, I wrote a jingle to the

tune of "The Hokey Pokey." Then I threaded the charms
on my laces, threw on my jogging clothes and drove to the
McDonald's head office.

Shamelessly, I used my previous connections to get an
appointment with the president. During my married life,
I'd once met George Cohon at a dinner party. I wasn't even
sure he'd remember me, so I wasn't prepared for his reaction
when I jogged into his office, waving my feet in the air and
singing my jingle: "You put your SHOE-MACs on . . ."

"Man, Miss Plum!" he said, clearly charmed by my laces.
"You made these?" He was chewing gum, sifting through
the piles of extra charms and laces I'd just thrown onto his
desk. "Jeez!" Then he grinned broadly and started punching the buttons on his phone. "Get me Jack! Get me Kathy!"
When his assistants rushed into his office holding steno
pads, he threw the laces at them and pointed to my charm-
laden shoes. "You gotta see these!"

He turned back to me. "Tell you what!" he said. "We'll
order a million of 'em . . . and if they take off in Canada,
we'll get you into the States." He whistled through the space
between his two front teeth. "This could be big!"

I rushed back to my car in high excitement, thinking
finally someone believed in my creativity. All I needed to do
was get my charms made for five cents or less and reap the
penny profit. But I hadn't done my homework. I hadn't
secured a factory. If McDonald's was talking about a million
pieces or more, I'd need some help.

I phoned my old colleague Ed, from Simpsons-Sears. I remembered he'd worked with a supplier for Disney, and I wondered if they had a factory I could use.

"Wait!" said Ed, as if he hadn't heard me correctly. "Are you telling me you just got a premium order from McDonald's?"

"Only an initial order . . . for a million pieces."

Ed was silent for so long that I thought he'd dropped the phone. "Uh, uh, but how did . . . uh, uh, do you realize how rare this is?"

"I know," I said. "That's the problem. I didn't expect to get the order same day."

"Same day?!"

"I thought they'd have to think about it. I thought I'd have time to find a factory."

"Listen," said Ed. "My guys have been trying to get a premium into McDonald's for *three years*! Hang tight. I'll make the call for you right now." As he hung up, I heard him mutter, "They're never gonna believe this!"

Ed was right, his guys were excited. They wanted to copartner. But weeks went by, and even with all their clout, they couldn't find a factory to manufacture my charms for under six cents. The shoelaces were no problem, that they could do, but machines capable of printing multiple colors onto uneven plastic surfaces didn't exist. The charms would have to be hand-painted. The cost was prohibitive. They assured me they'd find another solution. They weren't going to let a potential order from McDonald's slip through their fingers.

Three months later, I was back in their boardroom, turning over their samples in my hands. They'd printed pictures of hamburgers and fries on flat plastic discs. What kid would want to collect those? There was no movement, no adventure, none of the excitement of my childhood cannon ring. They looked like the kind of ID tags that tennis clubs handed out to members for free. Embarrassed and crestfallen, I had the uncomfortable task of admitting defeat to McDonald's. I couldn't deliver. I berated myself for thinking I could earn a living off my ideas. None of them ever got off the ground, not my idea for an automatic sailing mast when I was ten, not my idea for a handheld sewing machine when I was in high school nor any of my inventions since then, including my brilliant convertible pram. My head was always bursting with ideas, but what good was it? I'd even designed my resumé as a pack of cards and received not a single job offer. It was time I grew up, quit playing and looked for a "real" job, one with regular hours and a steady paycheck. After all, Dad always said, "Life isn't meant to be *easy*."

I'D HEARD FROM A FRIEND that United Flowers by Wire was looking for a creative director. When I went for my interview with the president, I was honest. Although I loved flowers and believed they had souls, I told him I didn't really know the first thing about them. I even confessed that most houseplants died under my supervision. The only one I couldn't kill was something called mother-in-law's tongue, a tough, scary plant I'd received during my marriage, which continued to grow no matter how much I ignored it. Even after I'd stashed it in our garage, hoping to freeze it into submission, its tentacles had slowly snaked around the rafters and began heading towards our bedroom window like something out of a horror movie. I told him that I'd sold it at our garage sale.

The president said he didn't care. I didn't need to know anything about flowers. He was looking for someone who could "tell a story." He wanted me to write copy, oversee photography and print the catalogues. My glowing references from Sears had won him over. He wanted me to start immediately.

For the first few months, I loved the job. I was earning a decent salary, holding photoshoots at the florist shop around the corner in the King Edward Hotel, adding to my knowledge about catalogue layouts and printing techniques that I'd absorbed at Sears and learning corporate marketing strategies from the president, who seemed happy to mentor me. But as the year wore on, the reality of working *two jobs simultaneously* proved daunting. How could I be a full-time mother plus a full-time creative director?

School days ended at three p.m., but I didn't get home until six. What was I supposed to do with the three-hour gap? The cost of after-school care was prohibitive, even if I could find any, and trying to coordinate a patchwork of part-time babysitters or transportation to after-school programs seemed impossible, like trying to stop a chain of dominoes from falling, especially when one of my children got sick or the babysitter canceled. I knew that many "latch-key kids" were going home after school to empty houses, letting themselves in with a key. Parents who could afford it were abdicating their role to so-called nannies, although many nannies were young girls from overseas with no training whatsoever. They were also underpaid; we often paid more per hour to park our cars.

School holidays were of a different magnitude altogether: My three weeks' vacation didn't even cover Christmas and March Break, much less the summer, when schools were closed for two months. One hundred years after the industrial revolution, why were children still getting summers off? Was it to help with the harvest? One theory was that school buildings were too hot in the summer. But air conditioners existed now. Hadn't anyone told the school board? How could school hours be so at odds with a parent's working life? Why didn't schools operate all year long, like parents did?

Despite being exhausted at the end of my workday, I was expected to race through evening meals like a short-order cook before jumping in the car to chauffeur children to ballet classes, piano lessons or swim meets. In the mornings, I raced against the clock trying to make breakfast and fill lunch boxes at the same time. I longed for the invention of food patches. They were already available for nicotine, why not scrambled eggs? Or how about edible paper? I visualized rolls of paper impregnated with peanut butter hanging inside the front door, where the children could simply rip off a piece as they ran out the door.

Quality time had become the new buzzword. I suppose it was coined to rid working parents of our guilt, but we all knew children needed *quantity* too; we just didn't have it to give.

I agreed with Mum that parenting was the most important career on earth. What could be more important than raising the next generation of human beings? But society seemed not to care. There was no training and certainly no salary. What would happen, I wondered, if governments guaranteed a salary equivalent to that of a bank manager to stay-at-home mothers (or fathers)?

Conflicting voices raged in my head. One gave me the feminist pitch: *You can have it all!* The other sounded an alarm: *Okay, but who will raise the children?* Popular books claimed it "took a village," but where was the village? Old villagers were no longer at home, sitting on their stoops, keeping a watchful eye. They were either still working themselves or fleeing to adults-only retirement resorts in Florida. Raising children seemed to be a skill no one valued anymore. How could we acknowledge such a thorny issue without putting mothers back in the kitchen? Even the feminists tried to ignore it. In the sixties, we thought we could fling off our aprons and change the world, but here we were, twenty years later, and what had changed? Biology trapped us every time. Men didn't seem to have the same problem. At work, they had a secretary. At home, they had a wife.

The Pied Piper

☥

WITHIN A YEAR, PC had found a new partner—another single mother with three children. This would be her third marriage, and it was sobering to realize that another woman, after so much experience, had decided that PC was the perfect man.

Finding my new partner wouldn't be so easy. I wanted a romantic relationship, but I didn't want to remarry. Obviously, I had some baggage, but I looked for a man without any—preferably a childless widower. In my mind's eye, he was a crazed romantic with great derring-do, perhaps a flamboyant composer, someone who'd build me my creative barn at the bottom of his garden, leave me alone during the day and fling me across his piano at night.

There was no shortage of men. Only a shortage of time. I dated a British horticulturalist, an Argentinian filmmaker, a Canadian lawyer, an Albanian journalist and a Belgian sculptor. One evening, I got so fed up trying to cram all of them into my day-timer that I threw up my hands and invited all five to my house for dinner. I wanted to see them side by side, hoping it might help me choose one. Only four of them came, but instead of entertaining me, they spent the evening sparring with each other in such a weirdly macho way that they became characters I didn't recognize.

One night in 1981, friends invited me to a Christmas party. The sidewalks of the city were piled with snow, and inside their sophisticated townhouse, every room was festooned with wreaths and candles and twinkling lights. The place was packed, their foyer heaped with coats and boots, and everyone was jostling elbows in a cheerful mood. Midway through the evening, someone suggested we put our coats back on and parade into the neighborhood to sing Christmas carols. They began handing out musical instruments and noisemakers: tambourines, triangles, dented pots and pans with spoons. I'd been given a rusted harmonica that made no noise, and as we crowded outside, I laughingly shouted to no one in particular, "How can I sing with this?"

A tall guest with a maroon scarf knotted around his neck grabbed the instrument out of my hand, tossed it over his shoulder into the snowbank and whispered, "I'll give you something that'll make you sing!" He threaded his arm through my mine and tugged me away, shouting, "C'mon!" His warm breath puffed a little white cloud into the sky.

Luring me away from the party, he pulled me towards a busy intersection, where a row of shops were open late. Outside a florist, he said, "Close your eyes! Wait here!" In less than a moment, he was back, his eyes dancing with mischief. With a dramatic flourish, he whipped a long-stemmed red rose from beneath his coat and said, "Voila! May I introduce myself?" Then he threw back his head and laughed, sounding more musical than any of the instruments we'd been given.

I was instantly smitten. Zan was the kind of man I'd dreamt of—the crazed romantic who lived life as theater. A dramatic, hot-headed Frenchman, he'd traveled the globe as an architectural designer, laughing at life's absurdities. We shared the same interests in just about everything— books, art, film, theater, music and fashion—and his creativity electrified me. He was inventing modern furniture I'd never seen before; his prototypes cast in sleek aluminum received glowing reviews in architectural magazines. Over the following year, we wrote songs together, scoured flea markets for outrageous costumes to wear and tilted at windmills. He was a rule-breaker, which scared me and lured me simultaneously.

What I didn't know then was that Zan was battling an

internal, existential crisis. He'd been married and divorced, but years earlier, he'd lost a young son in a tragic skiing accident, and now, about to turn fifty, he was beginning to question everything in his life. Looking back, perhaps it was I who triggered his crisis—another impossible choice that forced his hand—but he tipped me into a journey of self-discovery, too. Shocked, I watched a downward spiral begin to engulf him. Turning his back on responsibilities, he ignored his debts for many months, till his business teetered on the edge of bankruptcy. When his beloved country house caught fire in a lightning strike and burned to the ground, he saw nothing but ruin.

"I can't breathe," he cried. He wanted to escape, to leave all his insoluble problems behind and take an extended break, possibly to Europe, possibly for a year. I knew I'd miss him. A year seemed so long, but I didn't want to stand in his way. I adored him too much. "Direction doesn't matter," he said. "My God has no *d* . . . I just need to *go*!"

He began selling everything, his burned-out property, his belongings, what was left of his business. There were so many threads to unwind, he couldn't sleep. In the mornings, his hands began to shake. Together, we chose his new motor-cycle, a bright-red Honda Gold Wing, and studied maps of Europe. He bought a cheap one-way passage on a Polish cargo ship leaving in late October. "I've done it now," he whispered into my ear. "It can't be undone." I hugged him. Buried my face in his neck. Inhaled his scent. "I'll write," he promised. "I'll send for you."

His first letter, postmarked Mâcon, France, begged me for understanding. "If I hurt you," he wrote, "I am so sorry. Leaving felt like a violent, tearing agony, like a giant elastic band stretched to the limit. As I left the harbor, it snapped, and I thought, what have I done? I wept."

As he began to travel farther south, towards the sun, his mood brightened. He described all the young people he was meeting: "You must know how happy it makes me to have contact with the young. I meet no one my age. They're probably all working away somewhere, waiting for holidays to arrive. I wonder if I'm crazy sometimes. Well, I guess I want to be crazy! It seems everything I've done in the past has turned to salt. You know how I hate salt!"

When he arrived in Spain, he visited the Alhambra, overlooking the valley of Granada, backed by the snow-covered mountains of the Sierra Nevada, and described the view as he peered through the Moorish windows into the valley below. "It's an earthly paradise—flowers, fountains and vistas to make your heart tremble."

He wrote of going to clubs late at night to watch flamenco dancers and one night coming across a young man in a courtyard who was playing his guitar and singing ancient Moorish tales, wooing his beloved in the balcony above. The singing woke the neighbors, and soon they all began emerging onto their balconies to bear witness and applaud. "What a night to be alive!" he wrote. "I don't walk back to my hotel, I float. How I would have loved to share this moment with you."

Every week for the next four months, I received increasingly lengthy handwritten letters filled with wonder at what he was seeing, and I clung to the hope that he was finally healing. I missed him and spent my lonely evenings typing his letters up, convinced they would make a great film script. In my usual trap of trying to fix other people's problems, I thought that if I could just help him become a scriptwriter (or why not a movie star?), perhaps his crisis would come to an end. I didn't stop to examine why I was willing to spend the good part of a year trying to kickstart his life instead of my own writing career. He hadn't asked for my help.

Norman Jewison's office wasn't too far from my house, so in early February, without telling Zan, I packaged up my twenty-page script proposal and dropped it off at Yorktown Productions on Gloucester Street. In my cover letter, I explained that Zan's escape through Europe on a motorbike would make a fantastic film—it was every man's midlife-crisis fantasy!

"We follow his journey south to the Mediterranean, through France, Portugal and Spain, and finally to the Canary Islands," I wrote. "As dawn is about to break, he roars through the sleeping villages and up the volcanic mountainside, aiming for the highest peak. In a suicidal frenzy, he careens his bike around hairpin turns, screaming, 'Let me go-o-o!' But just as he reaches the top, the sun explodes over the horizon and he screeches to a stop, overcome by the beauty and hope of the vista below."

I titled the script *My God Has No D*.

Mr. Jewison was kind enough to invite me up to his office and gently explain that Zan's story would be of absolutely no interest to anyone.

Except to me, I thought. By then, I was fully invested. I wanted to be part of my soulmate's story, to help him heal and succeed . . . or to catch him if he fell. So, in February, when Zan sent for me, I flew to the Canary Islands.

BEFORE I LEFT FOR THE AIRPORT, Dad took me into his study. I could hear my children tap-dancing in the living room with Mum. Before they'd even taken their suitcases upstairs, she'd cranked up her record player. Gene Kelly was crooning "Singin' in the Rain"!

"Thanks for looking after the kids while I'm away, Dad."

"Quite all right. Your mother's looking forward to it." He went to his desk and pulled out a letter written on his good stationery. "I want to give you something. It's a letter of introduction." Opening his leather-bound address book, he began copying down a name. "This is my good friend Dr. Stanley Pavillard. I think you've heard me speak of him before. He lives in Las Palmas, near the botanical gardens."

I certainly knew the name. Dr. Pavillard was the Dutch doctor who'd been in Malaya when the Japanese invaded in 1941. Dad had escaped, but Dr. Pavillard was taken prisoner and worked in the jungle camps near the Burma Thailand Railway made famous in the film *The Bridge Over the River Kwai*. Dad had often described Dr. Pavillard's heroism, how he refused to escape when he had the chance, choosing instead to stay behind to treat the sick and wounded. Dr. Pavillard had earned the nickname "Bamboo Doctor" by performing the first one-to-one blood transfusion in the prison camp using a hollow piece of bamboo. His many medical innovations saved the lives of countless POWs.

"Now, don't lose this," said Dad, carefully folding the paper and handing it to me. "If you ever need anything . . . anything at all . . . you call him. I'll let him know you're coming."

At Gran Canaria Airport, Zan was waiting for me. We hadn't seen each other for almost half a year. I saw his handsome, tanned, smiling face, his tousled hair and his leather bomber jacket, and I leapt into his outstretched arms. As I climbed onto the back of his motorcycle, I remember thinking, *What the hell am I doing? I've left three kids back home. If I die, Mum will kill me!* Naively, I thought the danger was on the road.

"Trust me," Zan shouted. "Hold onto my waist! When I lean into a curve, you lean in with me."

Roaring away from the airport, we followed the coastline road that twisted and turned through shape-shifting sands. Simultaneously terrified and exhilarated, I clung on, trying to remember which way to lean. I'd never been on a motorbike before. Zan kept shouting and signaling with his hands, but I couldn't hear a thing inside my helmet.

By late afternoon, we'd arrived at Zan's tiny one-bedroom apartment in the sunny, whitewashed town of Las Palmas. Much to my surprise, he appeared to have a roommate. A surly young man was scowling at me, snatching books and memorabilia from the window ledge and throwing his clothes into a duffel bag. Zan dismissed him with a wave of his hand and immediately took me to a restaurant where his other new Spanish friends were already seated around a long communal table. I was struck by their youth. Most were artists in their early twenties: painters, poets and musicians fulfilling their compulsory two-year military service on the island; a few were tourists, but they were all talking excitedly about costumes. Zan interpreted for me, explaining that I'd arrived on the opening night of the famous Carnival held there every February. He seemed to be their ringleader, helping them decide what to wear that night. I watched as they hung on Zan's every word. They seemed mesmerized, captivated, as if they would follow him to the ends of the earth. Exactly as I was doing.

Our meal continued into the evening, after which all these young friends followed us into Zan's apartment to change into their costumes and apply each other's makeup. A handsome young man from Cuba asked if he could borrow some of my clothes. He rummaged through my suitcase, hauling out my sexy black bathing suit dotted with rhinestones, black pantyhose and high heels. Someone handed him a blond wig and lipstick, and I watched with fascination as he primped in front of the full-length mirror, looking like a swarthy Marilyn Monroe. Zan began dressing as a Swiss dog trainer in lederhosen, with a young man dressed as a poodle crouched on all fours and leashed to him. I felt like I'd been plopped onto the set of *La Cage aux Folles*, but without a costume, I'd become simply audience.

When we went outside, the air was warm and the dark night magical, lit overhead by a spray of stars. In the distance, all along the shoreline, hundreds of tents glowed from within, bouncing with the energy of cabaret music. As we ran down to the beach, I kept bumping into laughing drag queens in exotic, feathered costumes who were teasing and taunting the stern Spanish soldiers who stood at every corner with machine guns slung over their shoulders. The scene was surreal. Ahead of me, I sensed something mysterious: alluring yet unnerving, intriguing yet treacherous, as if we were all complicit in a decadent dance, precariously perched on the edge of oblivion, joining the sound of the sand being sucked rhythmically back and forth into the foam of an endless sea.

In the wee hours of the morning, Zan and I, exhausted, fell into bed.

The next afternoon while Zan was at his Spanish language class, I sat on the beach chatting with some of the boys I'd met the night before. When I asked where their girlfriends were, they said they were safely back in their villages and explained that strict Roman Catholic mores meant that young Spanish girls weren't available for sex before marriage. During their two years of compulsory military service, they told me it was easier to turn temporarily to each other and laughingly compared it to British boarding schools. I realized how naive I'd been—and what an education I was getting.

That night, I shared with Zan what I'd learned on the beach. I'd always thought of myself as an open and accepting person. I'd never understood society's hostile attitudes towards homosexuality—with all the hate in the world, why complain about people who love each other?—but I didn't have any gay friends and I realized I had no idea what bisexuality was, exactly. Was it a temporary choice—"allegiance due to expedience," as the boys on the beach had explained—or was it a permanent preference? Of course, I understand now that sexuality and gender identification can fall anywhere along a wide spectrum, but in 1982 terms like *gender fluid* and *nonbinary* hadn't entered our lexicon. I was just struggling to understand what I was seeing and sensing. *If Zan was sharing his apartment with another man*, I thought, *why was there only one bed?* And if we were in a committed monogamous relationship, why had his surly roommate scowled at me?

The more questions I asked, the more Zan struggled to explain. Finally, he told me that, for him, love was an emotional need that only a woman could satisfy, while sex was a physical appetite. I knew you could experience sex without love—I'd done it myself—but there seemed to be more that he wasn't telling me. Why had he sent for me? I was confused by the ambiguous subtext swirling beneath our relationship. I wanted clarity, but Zan kept talking in circles, using the word *enlightened*. This was a word I'd heard before, used by couples trying to justify their open marriages, and I'd seen the emotional destruction it caused.

The first night, Zan and I had fallen asleep exhausted, which I attributed to our late-night partying and my jet lag, but after our long discussion on this second night, we did the same thing. I felt hurt. And puzzled. I knew he loved me, so why wasn't he showing it the way he had back in Canada, especially after we'd been apart for so long? He had tenderly kissed me, tracing the contours of my face with his fingertips, but he'd fallen asleep with his arms around me, and I felt rejected.

Suddenly, in the middle of the night, he began thrashing and kicking, then moaning and crying, uttering words and phrases I couldn't make out. "Shhhh, shhhh," I whispered, rubbing his shoulders. "You're having a nightmare."

He leapt from the bed like a wounded animal and jumped onto the chair, clutching his knees and rocking back and forth, his face contorted with fear. "Oh, you're the lady! You're the lady! You're the lady in the lamp!" He was still half asleep. Obviously, my presence was shining a light on something, but what? On the third night, Zan confessed that he might have a urinary tract infection. He wasn't sure, but whatever it was, he said he didn't want to pass it on to me. Tired of his excuses, I pulled out Dad's letter and handed him the address of Dr. Pavillard's medical clinic in downtown Las Palmas.

Dr. Pavillard greeted me like the daughter of his long-lost friend and asked how long I was staying. I told him two weeks. When Zan returned to the waiting room, he looked chagrined. Dr. Pavillard had ordered blood tests and asked

Zan to abstain from sex until the tests came back. How long? The duration of my visit: two weeks.

I never knew the results of his tests, but when I returned to Canada, I began to see news stories about a mysterious infection later called HIV/AIDS. In 1982, most of the information was coming out of Cuba, reported in the *Miami Herald* by investigative journalists in Florida. Unlike many countries that stigmatized the disease as a social issue affecting only homosexuals, Cuba treated it as a public health crisis. Suspected victims (sometimes along with their whole families) were immediately quarantined under medical supervision to track and try to stop the spread. Some of the cases were traced to Cuban soldiers who'd recently returned from duties in Africa. I remembered that the young Cuban who'd borrowed my clothes in Las Palmas told me he was taking a break from fighting in Angola, so I began to worry about Zan.

Those of us who came of age during the sixties were lulled into thinking sex was risk free. Penicillin and the Pill had changed everything and spawned the so-called free love movement. We no longer worried about dying from an STD like syphilis or a backroom abortion (if your father hadn't killed you first). We thought free love would last forever, but here we were, twenty years later, and suddenly it had deadly consequences.

I mailed Zan the newspaper clippings I'd collected, warning him to be careful, but he didn't react. Instead, he wrote that he was now reading *Report to Greco* by Nikos Kazantzakis, an autobiographical novel about personal crucifixion and resurrection. He may have thought of himself as "enlightened," but I was feeling more enlightened myself. Dating a charismatic and daring Pied Piper might have felt exhilarating at the beginning, but I wasn't prepared to follow him around the next dangerous curve. Over the following year, as we continued our letter-writing, I gradually surrendered my romantic expectations and our relationship evolved into a deep and abiding friendship . . . although one that would still provide some twists and turns.

JUST AS ZAN WAS RECEDING from my romantic life, I met the writer Merle Shain. She was a decade or so older than I was, and she was living my dream. Before we met, she'd been a journalist, magazine editor and television host. Now, she was living the life of a celebrated author. She was the only writer I knew, so I watched her habits with fascination, hoping I could learn how she did it. I'd abandoned the film script about Zan's midlife crisis and started a new novel of my own, a thriller set in Cuba about a corrupt pharmaceutical company using quarantined AIDS patients as human guinea pigs in their race for a cure.

I'd written the synopsis and a marketing plan and sent it to an agent, who promptly asked for a sample chapter. He sounded excited and said he was heading to New York to show it to a publisher. This was enough to activate all my insecurities (what if my sample chapter wasn't *good* enough?), and I quickly shelved the project before I was exposed as an imposter. Becoming a published author was the loftiest dream I had, the dream I'd held since I was five years old, but how could I mount those towering steps? I had no idea how to do it, even when somebody opened the door at the top and said come on up! To earn a living, I was still writing advertising copy for floral catalogues.

Merle made writing—and getting published—look effortless. She wrote in bed, propped up on lacy cushions, scribbling her thoughts about life and love onto tiny scraps of paper, plumbing the depths of her friends, like me, for material. She'd already had a wildly successful debut with *Some Men Are More Perfect Than Others* and followed it up with *When Lovers Are Friends*. Her publisher was begging her to write more books.

Whenever we talked, her subject was men. I complained that none of my dates captured my imagination the way Zan had, and furthermore, whenever I did meet any interesting men, I'd discover they were married. She waved away my concerns. "Don't worry," she said. "If you live long enough, you can have any man you want. All you need to do is outlive their wives!" Apparently, a girlfriend of hers had moved into a ritzy retirement home and within a few years had married four times: Her trick was to outlive the husbands, as well. But I didn't want to move into a retirement home. I was only thirty-five years old.

In the spring of 1983, when Merle was nearing completion of yet another book, we drove together to Letchworth State Park in upstate New York for a weekend getaway. Situated on the banks of the Genesee River, William Letchworth's original nineteenth-century mansion was now the Glen Iris Inn. The charm was still there—the faded wallpaper, creaky wooden floorboards and chintzy upholstery—but the glory was gone. Tourists hadn't discovered it yet. As we drove along the winding path, deep into wooded parkland, it was easy to feel like we'd entered an enchanted realm. Our double room had two four-poster beds and its own private balcony overlooking the river.

By mid-afternoon, we'd settled outside, lounging in wicker chairs on the flagstone terrace, surrounded by tall trees. Merle had offered to help me dissect my relationship with a new man over the weekend, trying to protect me from myself, as girlfriends often do.

Behind us in the gulley we could hear the rampant river as it rushed and tumbled into a spectacular waterfall before breaking itself over the rocks. As I continued to moan about the current man I was dating, the inn's receptionist kept running over to tell us that there was yet another long-distance call for Merle in the lobby. Her publisher was trying to negotiate terms, and her tactic was to sweetly delay until she got what she wanted. What she wanted this time was for the endpapers to be printed in a William Morris design, which the publisher said would be too expensive.

Merle was a tough negotiator, but she presented as a fragile bohemian. Still shopping for a husband herself, she regularly dressed in white, like a ready-made bride. Over a long white flounced skirt, she wore a wispy white smock edged in antique lace, belted with ties that dangled with turquoise beads. A wide-brimmed straw hat framed her delicate face. Dark bangs fell into her eyes.

"You're drowning yourself in this man," said Merle finally, jotting down notes, as she often did when we talked. "So, I have a question: If you insist on drowning, why are you choosing such shallow water?"

That line, I suspected, would make it into her next book, which it did, but why blame the water? The bigger question, which none of us asked, was why women were still waiting to be rescued by a man, Merle included? We knew the cost. To turn ourselves into props for men was soul-destroying. Those of us born in the thirties and forties were supposed to know better. Supposedly, we could be anything we wanted to be. Our grandmothers had won us the vote. Our mothers had fought for our freedom. In Canada, we'd even been declared persons in 1929!

So, what was my problem? Lust?

THE FOLLOWING VALENTINE'S DAY, I woke up and looked out the window. It was typical weather for February in southern Ontario: cold, gray and depressing. There was no man in bed to indulge me, but since I'd always been able to enrich my life with fiction, I imagined myself slithering out of a sexy silk camisole, being sprayed with Eau de Joy, and dribbled with melted chocolate from Fouquet's in Paris.

Suddenly, a tiny flurry of footsteps broke my reverie. Suppressed giggles filtered through the crack under my bedroom door and . . . just like the part in Cinderella when the mice sing and dance and fashion a dress out of nothing . . . the door burst open. With the best of intentions and love in their hearts, the oldest two mice shoved a plate of burnt toast under my nose, while the youngest heaved a two-gallon jug of antifreeze onto my bed. Apparently, she'd cashed in all the free coupons she collected whenever her father took her to the car wash. Thirty years earlier, I'd made my own mother macaroni earrings on just such a day and watched with pride as she wore them to church, but I decided that this was the last Valentine's Day I'd wake up to a present of antifreeze. I wanted company: adult male company.

Under the misguided notion that I might be able to do better than I had before (not a better man, just a better match), I ventured into the world of "Companions Wanted." Today, a prince logs onto a dating website or simply swipes right on Tinder, but in 1983 when I was scrubbing the hearth, he took out an ad in the classified section of the national newspaper.

One day, after sending the mice off to school, I sat down with my coffee and read the following: "To young women wishing to find love with class. Four outstanding European bachelors with chivalric titles, large ancestral chateaux, lakes, forests and farms seeking four outstanding marriage-minded single ladies, max.33."

I read exactly what you just read, but what I *heard* was "the Duke has issued a proclamation!" I knew I was older than thirty-three and certainly not a "single lady," but I decided the ad was a joke. Obviously, this was simply one clever prince with a great sense of humor trying to increase his odds. Whoever wrote this fiction deserved a reply in kind! Besides, the timing was perfect. The return address was a PO box in Montreal and Zan had just moved there and invited me to come visit him. Tumbling over the watershed between reality and fantasy, I spent two days composing a response, mashing together every bit of saucy material I could remember from my past romances, including some from Zan, Pierre and PC. (I typed it on my little red typewriter, which had a particularly enchanting font.)

Darling,
Remember our breakfast at the Hotel des Bergues in Geneva? (It was the first time I'd ever seen oranges the color of blood-red sunsets!) Or the time we lined up for hours in Tuscany waiting for the hydrofoil to take us to Elba where we danced all night at that disco in the mountains and the ceiling was open to the stars? When you left me at the Olivetti's in Costa Smeralda, I cried for three hours. But then you promised to show me the black sands of Lanzarote and the Carnival in Las Palmas! And while we were dancing at El Coto, the tiny art deco compact you gave me (the one with your telephone number engraved on the back) fell out of my bag, and I haven't been able to find you since!

I'm sorry this is such short notice, but when I saw from your ad that all four of you were in Montreal, I had to let you know that my itinerary will take me there next weekend. I'll be an artist at some crazy disco called Les Foufounes Electriques. Apparently, I paint for an hour and then they auction me off—wet!

x-Cherie

P.S. I'll be wearing those red cardboard earrings you made for me last Valentine's Day. One of them fell apart so I'm enclosing the pieces in the hopes you can fix it when I see you.

As soon as I'd finished typing, all my ugly stepsisters chimed in. Unlike Cinderella's, mine were in my head, other facets of my own personality, itching to remind me how undeserving I was.

You? they shrieked. *You think the prince wants* you? And they howled mercilessly as the mice scattered around the kitchen demanding to be fed, knocking over the macaroni and mashing their coleslaw between the cracks in the linoleum.

Trailing the phone cord behind me, I closeted myself in the downstairs bathroom to call Merle. She had begun starring as the Fairy Godmother in my Cinderella delusions, alongside my ugly stepsisters and the mice.

"You won't believe what I've just done," I whispered into the receiver. "Listen to this!" I read her the newspaper ad. "What do you think? It's got to be a joke—right?" Then I read her my letter. "Should I send it?"

"It's fucking fantastic!" said Merle, who had just finished writing *Hearts That We Broke Long Ago*. "If you don't mail it, I'm going to send it to *The New Yorker*. Either way, you've got a ready market!" In Cinderella's day, men were known as "beaux" or "courtiers" or "one's intended." But in 1982, as my fairy godmother reminded me, we called them "ready markets."

My friend Jeanette, the costume designer I'd met at York University, rushed right over. It helps to have a large cast of creative friends if you're planning to dramatize your life, and Jeanette was already selling her whimsical, two-dimensional cardboard earrings at the Art Gallery of Ontario. She acted like it was the most normal request in the world to desecrate one of her masterpieces. Carefully breaking apart one of her heart-shaped earrings, she handed the pieces to me and I popped them into the envelope, using Merle's return address for anonymity.

Two weeks later, I boarded the train for Montreal, leaving the mice behind with their father. I didn't care how many car washes they'd have to suffer through. CN trains were notoriously late in those days and the similarity to the pumpkin did not escape me, so I arranged to arrive well before midnight. Zan met me at the station with an affectionate hug. It seems I'd effortlessly moved him from his original starring role as the Pied Piper, where he didn't work out, to a supporting role as the coachman in a

Cinderella story, where he fit perfectly. (See how confusing fairy tales are?)

The thought flitted through my brain that perhaps I was being unfair to him. After all, he was the one who'd invited me for this weekend, long before I'd taken the script into my own hands and added this subplot. My request to be an artist at Les Foufounes Electriques (Zan called it Foufs) had been denied, he told me. In fact, he was surprised I'd asked him to arrange it, but he agreed to go with me just for fun, as a spectator. When my conscience kicked in (how could I have tricked the Pied Piper into driving me to the ball?), I decided not to wear Jeanette's other heart-shaped earring. I lost my nerve. My ugly stepsisters were having a field day.

In Montreal's Latin Quarter, Foufs was dark and dingy, nothing like the palace ball I'd imagined in my script. Walls were painted black, and pulsating rock music blared from the speakers. We pushed our way in, past hordes of pale, thin, androgynous voyeurs in black leather jackets, many with shaved heads and silver bullets riveted up the sides of their ears. A few had bull rings in their noses. One crazed wraith in the middle of the room was wafting beer bottles back and forth like incense, sloshing sticky bubbles all over the floor.

Twenty identical large, white canvases hung on the walls around the perimeter of the room, and artists knelt beside them, setting up their tables with brushes, rollers, palette knives and paint. Hard light from naked bulbs shot down from the ceiling as the thudding music pumped faster and faster. Crowds of spectators jostled for space.

The master of ceremonies grabbed the microphone. I'd noticed his name with expletives had been spray-painted in graffiti on the ladies' room wall. "You 'av une heure!" he screamed. "Un! Deux! Trois!" As an automatic timer ticked down, the performing artists whipped into action, rolling, smearing and splattering their paint. The crowd surged wildly from one canvas to the next. Suddenly, a shout went up. Excited hands pointed to a corner where an artist had brought his girlfriend as a prop. She was disrobing, undulating in the nude to the throb of the music. Using slow, deliberate strokes with a wide housepainter's brush, the artist bathed her in red paint, carefully outlining her genitals in "Klein Blue" that trickled down the inside of her thighs. The crowd went crazy, pushing and shoving. He threw her body against the canvas, leaving abstract blobs of a human form, then stood back to admire his art. He pressed her again: an elbow here, a toe there.

The late French performance artist Yves Klein had staged similar performances decades earlier, but I guessed this wannabe "protégé Parisien" thought he'd belatedly bring his ideas to Montreal. I stood transfixed, having long since forgotten about the prince. An hour passed. The timer buzzed, and the bilingual MC screamed, "Arrêtez! Stop!"

Crowds began roaming past the canvases, previewing the art, waiting for the auction to start. The band had softened, changing its tune. Zan went off in search of some drinks. As I turned to watch him go, I froze in disbelief. There—less than three feet away—stood a tall, impeccably dressed gentleman in a felt fedora, three-piece suit and black cashmere overcoat. His arms were folded across his chest, and he was hugging a brown manila envelope with handwriting on the front that was . . . undeniably . . . mine! My ugly stepsisters huddled in the corner of my brain, too stunned to speak.

I placed my hand on the gentleman's shoulder, stood on my tiptoes and whispered in his ear, "I'm not wearing my heart-shaped earring, but I think the person you're looking for is . . . um . . . me."

"*Ahhh,*" he said, looking me up and down with an expression of relief. "Then you are not la peinture?"

I shook my head. Did he really think I was the one with my genitals outlined in blue ink?

"I 'av your other ear-ring!" he said, grinning. He held out Jeanette's red cardboard heart. It dangled from its ear clip. Amazingly, he'd fixed it.

"I recognize m-m-my envelope," I said, feeling faint and looking around for Zan. "But please, put that away. I'm here with a friend!"

"Ah, I see." He hastily tucked the envelope inside his coat.

"I can't talk to you now," I whispered. "But I want you to know that I thought your ad was brilliant." I smiled knowingly. "In fact, I knew it was a joke."

See? screeched my ugly stepsisters. *It doesn't fit! It doesn't fit! It doesn't fit!*

"Au contraire!" He bowed his head courteously. "C'est très sérieux. I am the intermédiaire. I 'av been sent by the four ba-che-lors to meet you, mam'selle."

He's good, I thought. *Very good. Still playing this charade with a French Canadian accent.* But he didn't look like the imaginative type. Was he in disguise? Where was the figment of my imagination? I needed to buy more time until I figured it out.

"Did you get a good response?" I asked, trying to distance myself now, trying to sound professional, sluicing my previous marketing career for appropriate jargon.

But you clean hearths! screamed my ugly stepsisters.

He shrugged. "About four-tee réponses. Surtout stupide." He waved a dismissive hand. "Too *intellectuel*. Pfft!"

A familiar hand slid up my back. I stiffened and blushed and turned to find Zan, who had returned with two beers. Looking suspiciously at the interloper, he grabbed my hand and tugged me away. "C'mon!" he said. "There's something I want to show you."

I looked back at the intermediary, who was trying to shout above the din. "You 'av been see-lec-teed, mam'selle. You must take this!" He waved a second envelope at me, a large, white one.

I shook my head, thinking, *How can I take your glass slipper, when I'm here with my old friend the Pied Piper?* Over my shoulder I yelled, "You'll have to mail it!"

"Very well . . . I weel mail eet!" As he disappeared into the crowd, I heard him shout, "Congratulation, eh?"

"What's with that guy?" said Zan.

"Part of a subplot," I said and grinned. "I'll tell you later." I knew he'd understand my fantasy since he suffered similar delusions of his own, and later that night, when I told him the story, he roared with laughter.

At the train station the next morning, he gave me a gentle kiss on the cheek. "Now don't talk to any strange men."

"You mean, don't answer any more ads."

"Answer all the ads you want. Just let me know when the mail comes. I want to know how it ends!"

Five days later, Merle phoned me. "Get over here quick," she squealed. "It's arrived!"

She'd spent the morning writing in bed, so when I banged on her door, she greeted me in a long, white Victorian nightdress, her dark hair pulled into a messy bun poked with chopsticks. We ripped open the large, white envelope and emptied the contents onto her glass-topped coffee table. Out tumbled documents and dozens of photographs. Four crumbling castles were in various states of disrepair, two surrounded by moats. There were close-ups of gargoyles and coats of arms; others showed deer gamboling through parklands.

"Fucking hell . . ." said Merle, "is this for real? There really are *four* bachelors?" She waved a sheaf of papers in my face. "Will you look at these?" She was squealing again, her already high-pitched voice notched up a few octaves. "They've even included their medical records!"

"Wait," I said, skimming the covering letter. "Listen to this! They all want good-looking, broad-minded wives with financial means!"

"Are you beginning to get the picture?" said Merle, laughing.

There were four separate CVs, each one numbered for anonymity. Bachelor #1 claimed to be a recognized international literary talent. Bachelor #2 was an engineer. Bachelor #3 was interested in botany. And Bachelor #4 wrote reassuringly that he no longer suffered the stresses of running a castle because he was now in marketing; he'd recently launched a business and moved to Toronto.

"Good God," shrieked Merle, pointing to his business address, "it's right down the street from your house!"

There was a three-page questionnaire for me to fill out, designed to sniff out my religious affiliation, my sexual persuasion and my willingness to produce heirs. What? Produce more mice? No, I decided—no, no, no.

But it was hard to abandon the script I'd already plotted in my imagination. For the next few weeks, the questionnaire sat on the shelf in my bedroom. I even started to fill it out one night when there was nothing good on TV. When it asked whether I lived alone or with roommates, I circled *roommates* and listed their ages as five, seven and nine. When it asked whether I felt "negatively about bisexuals," I knew this was a leading question. "I don't consider bisexuals negatively," I answered. "In fact, I usually fall in love with them. But I don't consider them positively as life partners for me."

After more than thirty questions, they asked for comments. I studied the talents of all the bachelors and wrote, "I suggest we redevelop all the castles into high-end condos. Bachelor #2 can design them, #3 can plant the gardens, #4 can market them internationally, and I'll help #1 write a book about it." They asked for a photo, so I attached one. Then I put the questionnaire back on the shelf.

Five days later, Merle phoned again. "You won't believe this," she said, "but there's another fucking letter!"

We'd underestimated the persistence of Bachelor #1. It turned out, I'd met him face-to-face, disguised as the intermediary. This time, Merle uncorked her best champagne, brought out a dish of truffles and put on her tortoise-shell reading glasses. She'd already opened his letter before I got there. In her best French Canadian accent, she began reading what can only be described as a disturbed love letter from a sick puppy who'd decided I was exactly what he was looking for. He claimed his tingling fingertips had absorbed my essence through the back of my original envelope.

"Ew-w," I said, "how creepy!"

My reluctance to send back their questionnaire only seemed to enhance my desirability. By the time his third letter arrived, insisting on a date, I was hyperventilating and Merle had tired of acting as my fairy godmother.

"This is nuts!" she said, pushing her glasses up over her bangs. "I don't care what kind of castle he has. This guy is just out-of-his-mind crazy. He likes to crunch glass with his teeth as a party trick, for God's sake! And he wants *heirs*!"

In the end, I took Merle's advice and told him my tubes were tied.

After a few more drinks, she collapsed on the sofa and looked at me sideways. "Tell me something. How come you never married Zan?"

"Because of the Canaries," I said.

"As in the black sands of Lanzarote, or the little fluffy yellow things you put down a mine shaft?"

"Both." I sighed. "I'll tell you one day."

Reinvention

MERLE OFTEN CLAIMED to be Ralph Lauren's muse. It was true she had a wonderful eye for design—especially when it came to fashion and home furnishings—but now she said she was tired of "giving away her ideas." She was itching to produce her own line of bed linens. We had often discussed entrepreneurial ideas together, and now she was urging me to leave my job at United Flowers by Wire to help her start a company. But home decor had never held any interest for me. A different idea was percolating in my mind.

In the evenings after work, as I waited in my car for my children to emerge from their extracurricular activities, I began making notes in a journal. I dreamt of creating local parenting magazines—resources for working parents in every city across the country that would offer advice and support. It was much like the *PikQuik Papers* I'd produced in college for my classmates. Perhaps it was time once again to make something out of nothing, to take a risk. I could use my copywriting skills from Sears and my newly acquired experience producing catalogues for United Flowers by Wire. With a publishing company, I could also work from home and have more flexibility when it came to my children's needs.

In my journal (called *Diary of a Waiting Chauffeur*), ideas spilled onto the page. I sketched the layout, the articles, the marketing strategy, even the distribution plans. I could literally see the first edition, not as some vague idea, but the actual thing, fully formed and successful—Canada's first parenting magazine.

At first, I tried to get funding support from the city but without success. I approached people in the magazine industry, but they said I was nuts. "A magazine for parents?" said one publisher. "It'll never work. You'll just be putting money down a black hole." But I'd learned in childhood that people don't get ideas, ideas get people, and this one had reached down from the ether and grabbed me and wouldn't let go.

Throughout the summer of 1983, I sought a start-up loan from the banks, but they required a husband to cosign, and I no longer had one. I had $10,000 in savings, and one bank offered to lend me $10,000 if I put up my $10,000 in collateral, but what sense did that make? Why would I pay interest on a loan when I could use my own money for free? The only black hole I could see was at the bank. There was only one option left—to use my own savings for initial costs, budget on a shoestring and break even from day one. I figured we could save rent by operating out of my house. Advertising revenue would pay for the printing. Each month, we'd print only as many pages as we could afford, and we'd distribute copies through the children's stores that advertised with us. All I needed was a sales force of intelligent, enthusiastic mothers who, like me, were looking for purpose. They'd work on commission, and the more mothers I could attract from different neighborhoods, the faster the word would spread.

On weekends in Oakville, while the children played with Mum, I sat at the dining room table with a calculator working out projected profits and losses on giant sheets of graph paper. Dad was impressed. He'd never seen me so interested in mathematics.

I quit my job at United Flowers by Wire and began searching for staff. Madeline Kronby was a writer and actress who ten years earlier had played Louise in CBC's long-running children's series *Chez Hélène*. She had useful contacts in the media world and was looking for work as an editor. I hired her on the spot. Soon, we were joined by Shauna Jones, a young friend of my brother's who'd been temping as a receptionist. She was a quick study—bright, energetic, organized and highly self-motivated—and within a few years Shauna would become my co-publisher.

In my unfinished basement, amidst the clanging pipes of
the boiler and the washing machine, we installed telephones
and secondhand typewriters, balancing old wooden doors
on top of filing cabinets to create desks. Upstairs, the dining
room became our sales office. Whenever the extra phone
lines rang, all three of us faked different voices—pretending
to be secretaries, receptionists or sales executives—as if we
were a thriving company with a cast of thousands. Soon,
the house was filled with laughing mothers, and my children
never returned from school to an empty house or to idle
hours before dinner; they were immediately put to work
stuffing envelopes. I was constantly trying to cut costs. With
no budget for couriers, we rerouted our personal errands
to accommodate deliveries. Business lunches were out of
the question, and instead of group health insurance, which
we couldn't afford, I provided a huge box of daily multivi-
tamin pills. The only thing left was to find our first major
advertiser. I knew this was crucial: We needed a high-profile
international company to lend authority and credibility and
encourage other advertisers to buy in.

Remembering George Cohon's encouragement two
years earlier, when I'd waltzed into his office wearing my
SHOE-MACs, I called McDonald's. Knowing they couldn't
justify buying an ad based solely on our small local circulation, I told him about Child Find, a U.S. charity that had
recently expanded into Canada and needed publicity. If
McDonald's bought our back cover each month to sponsor
an ad for missing children, I figured they could use the cost

TOP LEFT: Miss Alice with Dad and his sisters, 1917.

TOP RIGHT: Mum is the babe in arms in this row of eight siblings at Rokeby Farm, 1917.

LEFT: Mum took me to meet Dad for the first time in Hong Kong, 1947.

BOTTOM: Robin, me, Mum, Chris and Sandy on the lawn in Oakville, 1953. (Victor would be born two years later.)

IMAGINATIVE GENIUS AT WORK

TOP LEFT: Newly arrived in Canada: my first day at Miss Lightbourn's School, age 5.

TOP RIGHT: My brother Sandy, neighbor Steve Alcock and me: Oakville, 1953.

ABOVE: Drawn to theatre from an early age: age 11, staging a play at the Oakville Public Library.

RIGHT: Pierre's favorite picture of me, age 20 on the beach in Oakville.

TOP LEFT: My
brothers and I
putting on a skit
in the living room.

TOP RIGHT: Touring
as the Wicked Queen
in *Snow White*,
Boston, 1965.

ABOVE: My first leading
role in Mrs. *Dally Has a
Lover*, with Sean
Roberts, Boston, 1967.

RIGHT: As Madame
Bouffier in *Jacobowski
and the Colonel*; our
production won the Moss
Hart Award.

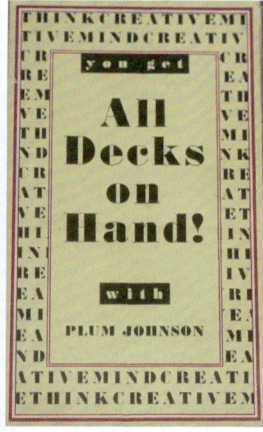

TOP LEFT: Headshots
for my TV auditions,
1980; one look at my
crooked teeth and they
said I'd never get a
leading role.

TOP RIGHT: My resumé
designed as a deck of
cards. It didn't result
in a single job offer!

ABOVE: The heart-shaped
earring that I mailed to the
Montreal bachelors.

RIGHT: A box of Photoballs
which we sold on The Shopping
Channel in 1996 (now a
collector's item!)

TOP LEFT: Shauna Jones and I in our Kids Toronto new offices, 1986.
TOP RIGHT: My brother Sandy helping me out at a trade show.
BOTTOM LEFT: We hired photographer Michale John Wood to take
celebrity photos for our covers—here are Shari Lewis and Lambchop.
BOTTOM RIGHT: An issue of *Help's Here!*, the magazine I co-founded
with Margaret Fleming in 2002.

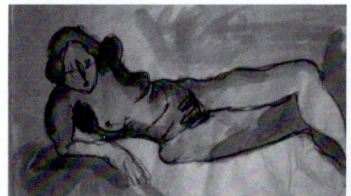

TOP LEFT: Three of the ink sketches I smuggled home from Robert Markle's life drawing classes around 1980.

TOP RIGHT: My self portrait, *She's a Real Dish* (2001), that Carter didn't want me to sell.

LEFT: The sampler I embroidered for Farah Khan as I watched the murder trial of her parents on TV in 2001.

RIGHT: Pat Goss came with me when I exhibited my portrait of her at an art gallery in Oakville, 2008.

BOTTOM RIGHT: Studying etching at the Falmouth College of Art, Falmouth, England, 2006.

BOTTOM LEFT: With my handmade papier maché faceplates, breastplates and fingerbowls.

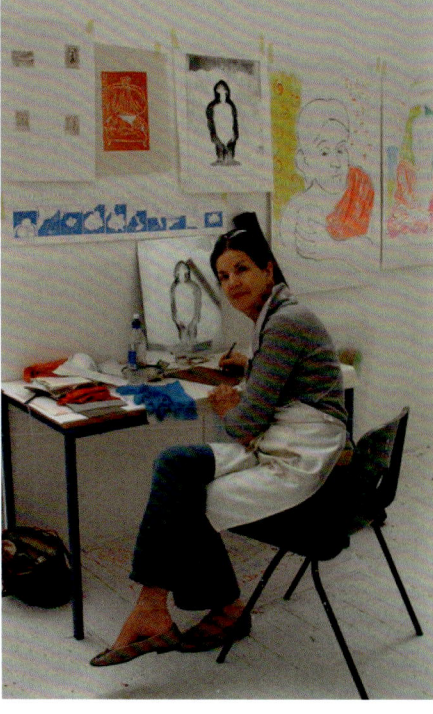

Dear Mrs. Johnson:

I am returning your manuscript "Down in the Dumps" for one reason only; we already have 3 books on garbage in our line. But your efforts are tremendous and I encourage you to do more and submit them to us.

Here are the comments from our senior children's editor to me: "Mrs. Johnson's verse is lively and amusing; we would be happy to see more of it if she has a manuscript dealing with something other than garbage. As you know, we have done a couple of rhyming LITTERBUG books, and I don't see a place now for another that teaches the same kind of lesson. Mrs. Johnson's lesson is very well done--and painless--however, and I hope she writes to us again."

These are very complimentary indeed and she, as do I, feel that you have an extremely creative talent.

I would like to thank you for the kind comments on the reception you received from us and I am very pleased we did nothing to dampen your enthusiasm.

I look forward to seeing more of your manuscripts and again, your talent is a real treat to see.

TOP: The "rejection" letter from 1974 that I found after Mum died. It gave me confidence forty years later to try again.
BOTTOM: People lined up to view the house in Oakville after *They Left Us Everything* won the RBC Taylor Prize.

as a tax deduction, earn goodwill from the community and everyone would benefit: Child Find, McDonald's and us. It was a win-win-win.

"You got it," said George, and he bought a twelve-month contract.

KidsCanada Publishing Corp. debuted on Father's Day, June 1984, with the launch of *Kids Toronto*. Our cover featured eight well-known city fathers in their pin-striped suits, avidly reading the first issue as they rode to work on the subway. I doubt any of them had ever seen the inside of the subway, but one of them was chairman of the TTC at the time, and he arranged for the photo shoot; the others gamely went along for the ride. Who could say no to supporting parenthood? Over time, all kinds of celebrities agreed to be on our covers, from the Toronto Blue Jays baseball team to prima ballerina Karen Kain and even political figures like David Peterson, the premier of Ontario, who posed with his wife and children. The year we won the marketing award, we put George Cohon on our cover.

The excitement of our entrepreneurial adventure was contagious. With our newly minted business cards, we began fanning out across the city, spreading the word and drumming up business. Every day, swarms of mothers met in my living room to strategize. Madeline and I researched and wrote the articles, our sales team of mothers sold ads, and Shauna helped with everything else: During deadlines, after I'd fed my children and put them to bed, Shauna and I often worked throughout the night, designing the layout and pasting typeset galleys onto pages laid out on the living room floor.

Working in close quarters eliminated the need for formal meetings and memos, since we overheard each other's conversations. It was a highly efficient way of working, and when we expanded two years later, I rented an open-concept space on a single floor for this very reason. Having an all-female staff also had its advantages. We understood the pressures of childcare and established the rule that you could take time off whenever you needed. Personally, I'd always chafed at the idea of responsible adults having to ask "permission" for time off at work. If we couldn't be trusted, why were we there? I hired some single women, too, and the rule was the same for them. If they needed a day off, they could take it, no questions asked; the rest of us would take up the slack. The policy boosted morale, created mutual respect and bonded the staff.

Limited resources forced us to be creative. When we couldn't afford the $1,200 booth at our first CNE trade show, we paid $500 for a derelict Canada Post van that was missing its engine, towed it on site, hired the artist Ian Leventhal to spray-paint it and had the best booth in the place.

One of our biggest annual expenses was the typesetting fees. If only I could eliminate this step, we'd increase our profit—but how?

In 1984, I'd read an article about Apple's revolutionary desktop computer called the Macintosh and began wondering if this could be the solution to our problem. I drove out to their distributor for a demonstration. It was only the size of a shoebox, but I was so impressed, I bought one. I was convinced it would allow us to eliminate typesetting fees altogether by producing the galleys ourselves! When it proved successful, Apple told us we were the first commercial newspaper in North America to try such a thing and they were so impressed, they donated two more computers to our publishing venture.

IT WAS A HEADY, EXCITING TIME, and although I was totally focused and thought I'd put all my romantic adventures behind me, I had no sooner launched the company than I met a man who owned a market research company. He lived around the corner, which suited me perfectly. When my cousin met him, she said he reminded her of my brothers and fit right in. It was true. Like Robin, Chris and Victor, Simon was big and tall and bearded, with a sensitive, creative nature. On my way to meet him for one of our first lunch dates, I saw him coming towards me on Yonge Street and I broke into a run, waving our Father's Day issue in the air, hot off the press. It wasn't yet the final product I'd envisioned— it was only eight pages long—but I was on fire.

"We did it! We did it!" I shouted, and he lifted me up in a fierce bear hug and swung me around in the air.

Initially, like many men in the eighties, Simon was skittish about committing to a permanent relationship again. A new expression, "the walking wounded," referred to shell-shocked men whose wives had left them and taken half their bank account. Meanwhile, divorced women seemed to have established new rules, but men weren't sure what they were. Simon had been married twice before and had three children. Although I told him that I wasn't interested in remarrying, he was suspicious and didn't believe me.

Early in our relationship, I suggested joining him on one of his business trips to New York City, which plunged him into a full-blown anxiety attack. It was our first joint holiday with comingled expenses, and instead of the casual fun trip I'd expected, it was fraught with emotional traps. When we arrived at our hotel, Simon seemed confused about which one of us should sign the hotel register, who should pay for theater tickets, even who should open a door and let the other go first. If I tried to do any of those things, he accused me of being aggressive. When we got home, I tried to mirror his behavior by drawing him a small cartoon zine: *Man's Illustrated Guide to That First Weekend Date*, subtitled *How to Handle an Assertive Woman*. To his credit, he laughed and began to relax, and our fondness for each other blossomed.

Both of us enjoyed going off the beaten track. I never liked taking the same path twice, and Simon was always keen to explore new roads. During the following year, we toured southern Ontario on weekends, each of us looking for a different kind of escape. Simon was hoping to buy a tiny one-bedroom cabin in the woods, where he could disconnect from his responsibilities as a father, while I was looking for a huge farmhouse with enough bedrooms to accommodate all six of our children on weekends, to recreate the expansive family atmosphere I'd experienced as a child in Mum and Dad's house by the lake.

One weekend, we found ourselves exploring Prince Edward County, a mostly agricultural region on the north shore of Lake Ontario about two hours east of Toronto. The moment we arrived, we fell in love with the landscape and the people. It seemed to have everything we were missing in the city—clean air, apple orchards, corn fields, sand dunes, secret coves and beaches and friendly people who took the time to get to know you. Driving down a dusty road near the lake, I spotted a sign on a fencepost: ANTIQUES FOR SALE.

"Stop! Stop! Simon, stop!"

Up the driveway, overlooking the lake, stood a huge dilapidated Victorian house covered in rusted tin siding. Broken gingerbread trim hung from its porches. A large wooden barn and stone outbuildings stood in the distance. We clambered out of the car and met the farmer. His dusty drive shed near the road was filled with antiques: old wagon wheels, butter churns, maple syrup molds, hooked rugs, crockery and tools of every description. Treasures piled to the rafters.

"How much do you want for that cookie jar?" I asked, pointed to a cherubic ceramic face with a straw-hat lid.

"That's a collectible," said the farmer, "thirty-five dollars should do it."

"It's chipped," said Simon.

"I know, but I love it!"

Just then, I noticed another sign leaning up against the fence. Grabbing Simon's arm, I whispered, "Look—this whole place is for sale!" The sign was pockmarked and faded, looking like it'd been there for years. "Let's find out the price!"

"Are you crazy? It's a wreck!"

But I'd always loved the potential of wrecks and, as we drove away, I couldn't get the farm out of my mind. Three miles down the road, we came across a cemetery and stopped the car to explore. Among the many sad headstones of young children who'd died during a typhoid epidemic in 1885, I noticed a name and called Simon over. "Look at this one—it's the same last name as yours!"

Convinced that the Fates had brought him home to ancestors he didn't even know he had, I insisted we call the real estate agent. Apparently, the property had been on the market for years, so the agent wasted no time; we booked an appointment that same afternoon. It took more than an hour to walk the property, down a rutted tractor path, past hay fields and through distant woods to where the pretty Black River meandered along the rear boundary, clusters of orange tiger lilies spilling over its banks. By the time we got back to the front porch, the sun was shining and Lake Ontario glistened in the distance.

I was smitten—I could hear the house calling to me. Simon, however, was still reluctant. He thought the whole thing was too big. But I felt emboldened. I knew I didn't need his permission; the price was one I could afford on my own. Our original idea, to find a retreat we could use together, had been only that—a pie-in-the-sky idea. We never anticipated finding one so quickly, so we'd never discussed the finer points, like how we would furnish it or who would pay for it.

That evening, as we huddled in our hotel room, I told Simon that if he didn't want to buy it, I'd buy it myself. That seemed to motivate his dominant male spirit, and after debating an offer, by the end of the weekend the deal was done. Finally, I had a man with a barn, even if it wasn't yet filled with art supplies. And it had five bedrooms, enough to accommodate all our children.

Over the next five years, the farm became our weekend getaway. We spent the first summer donning workman's gloves to peel the tin cladding off the exterior, exposing beautiful bones of board and batten. We lifted layers of linoleum off the floors upstairs, each floral pattern more ancient than the last and often insulated with old newspapers; on the second-floor landing, we stripped all the way back to 1910, revealing an old newspaper ad for a wringer washer.

We learned how to lift the trapdoor from the floor of the kitchen to deal with dead rats in the cistern, how to disinfect the water well in the barnyard by adding bleach and how to keep the woodstove stoked all night in the winter so the heat would rise through holes in the ceiling and warm the house. In the fall, mounds of dead flies accumulated on window ledges and feral stray cats made their home in the barn.

We furnished the place with iron bedsteads, mahogany dressers, flea-bitten rugs and overstuffed sofas found at country auctions, and we bought a tiny black-and-white television, which beamed in one station across the lake from upstate New York. We learned to recognize our phone's party-line ring—one long, two short—and just for fun, for $800, we bought a 1952 black Cadillac convertible that had once belonged to the Royal York Hotel. We stored it in the drive shed to use on weekends and loved thinking it may have once carried Queen Elizabeth and Prince Philip on a royal visit to Toronto.

The county was full of artists, dreamers from the city who'd come for its rugged beauty and inexpensive lifestyle. We made friends with glassblowers and potters and a struggling young couple next door who had started to plant a vineyard, convinced the microclimate could produce first class wine. They could barely afford to heat their old stone house, which was crumbling around them, but they splurged on rare grapevines imported from France, cupping the spindly plants with reverence in the palms of their hands. Unfortunately, nobody else thought vineyards could succeed in the county, and they struggled alone, unable to find investors. They were visionaries, about thirty years ahead of their time: the only ones who knew that Prince Edward County could become a world-renowned wine making region.

I LOVED THAT SIMON WAS a nonconformist, an adventurer and an explorer at heart, but some of his explorations made me nervous. He glommed onto New Age fads, like est, later known as The Forum, and communities like the freethinkers in Lily Dale, New York. There were experiments where you could walk over a bed of nails or curl into a fetal position and howl from the womb, all a bit too adventurous for me. But I'd been reading *The Magic of Findhorn* about the spiritual community on the shores of the Moray Firth in the north of Scotland, and I wanted to visit it. Although Findhorn began in a trailer park in the sixties, where hippies hoped to welcome extraterrestrials on a landing strip for flying saucers, it had developed into a thriving commune where people communicated with plants. Apparently, they were using the energy of pyramids to grow enormous flowers and vegetables, and I wanted to see if it was true. It appealed to my childhood belief that all living things possess unique languages, if only we could learn to decipher them.

We flew to England, rented a car and drove north towards Inverness. But instead of the lush Eden I'd imagined, with forty-pound cabbages growing under pulsating crystal pyramids, we found a barren, sandy landscape beside a garbage dump, near the noisy runway of a military airport. Still, I was hooked on the idea that there was some sort of mystical force at work. Why not? It felt like we were at the ends of the earth, surrounded by what the community believed were strange magnetic fields. The road also pulled me back to my genetic origins. Only a few hours east, north of Dundee, we found the tiny village of Udny, the home of Dad's ancestors during the War of the Roses in 1455. I had always known about our connection to Udny (it was Dad's middle name and appears as a surname in our old family Bible), but I hadn't realized it was so close by.

We drove back through England to the southern county of Wiltshire, where we followed the ancient trail from Salisbury to Avebury, stopping at Stonehenge along the way. I'd been to Stonehenge before as a teenager when there were no ropes to keep tourists at bay, when you could still clamber over the site, but I'd never visited the Avebury Rings, where smaller henges stalk the town. When I started walking across the fields towards the stones, I sensed a strange, buzzing energy. I didn't feel like myself. I felt agitated and upset, unable to shake the persistent feeling that one of the large, upright stones was in the wrong place. It was as if I'd been there before. I kept saying to Simon, "That's not right. That one shouldn't be there!" Later that night in a small B&B that dated to the sixteenth century, I had a vision of being a young girl in the Elizabethan era, looking out the window at Simon, who was lifting hay bales in the barnyard below. Had we known each other in a previous lifetime? It might explain our telepathic connection.

Ever since we'd met, I felt able to communicate with Simon from a distance, much as I had with Pierre. With Pierre, I felt that I'd been a "receiver," but with Simon, I felt I could "transmit." If I was in the city and Simon was at the farm, all I had to do was sit quietly and transport myself to his side. It felt like an altered reality. Even though I was hundreds of miles away in the city, my spirit felt concentrated inside the farmhouse, experiencing smells in the kitchen, the pictures on the walls and the creaks on the floorboards as I searched each room until I found him and urged him to call. Inevitably, he did. I never told Simon about this; it was my own private experiment, but I'd always been curious about what other people called "coincidence" or "synchronicity." To me, there was so much that science couldn't explain.

I was encouraging Simon to write a novel. As a joke for Christmas, I gave him a blank book to which I added a fully illustrated paper jacket. It had the synopsis of a thriller printed on the flyleaf, fake endorsements from famous authors on the back and my picture on the front cover, pulling his leg. But the joke was on me. I was still unaware that I was projecting and sublimating my own ambitions, just as my mother had done; still trying to encourage others to write by handing out blank books.

OVER THE NEXT FEW YEARS *Kids Toronto* became profitable and I began making plans to expand across the country, launching *Kids Vancouver* and *Kids Calgary*. Similar parenting magazines were now popping up across North America and female publishers in cities like New York and Chicago began calling us for advice. It reminded me of the lesson I'd learned as a child when the name Bach had flown through the window and into my head. Ideas were like seeds, waiting to drop down into fertile ground; people often got the same idea at the same time. Most of the publishers were mothers, and most women who've learned to raise children have learned how to be good collaborators. It occurred to me that if we all banded together, we could attract major advertisers by offering much larger circulations than any of us could provide individually. Coincidentally, a new organization was taking shape in the United States: Parenting Publications of America. Shauna and I flew to their conferences in New York and Chicago to share our concept.

But just as it looked like nothing could stop us, the tides turned. Our financing had always been precarious. We budgeted on a tightrope, carefully balancing profit and loss, but in the spring of 1987, we ran short of cash and couldn't pay our print bill. We had a huge summer issue planned with a circulation of 300,000 copies, and I knew we'd be profitable by September; I begged the printers to extend us some credit, but they declined. Our bank wouldn't give me an overdraft, either, even when I offered my house as collateral. They pointed out that I was a single woman with children, and they wouldn't let me risk the roof over my children's head. They wanted to pull the plug and take away my job instead.

I gathered my staff together and told them we might have to close. They were stunned. We'd all made huge sacrifices, often taking salary cuts in the past whenever we'd hit hard times, and Shauna had once even offered to loan me her own life savings. Devastated, they urged me to try another bank. I couldn't see why a new bank would back us when our current one wouldn't, but I gave it one last try.

At the CIBC, I made an appointment with the manager, Tom Horsley, and spread our financial records across his desk. Instead of the condescending, patriarchal attitude I'd encountered at our previous bank, Tom was respectful and prepared to be supportive. He studied our records thoughtfully and then called me in for a second meeting, where he gave me a smart, creative challenge.

"Look," he said, "you need an immediate capital injection of twenty-five thousand dollars and probably more in the future. I know nothing about the publishing business, but if you can get *half* that—from people in the industry— that'll tell me you have a viable business, and I'll back you." As I was leaving, he doubled down. "By the way," he said, "I don't want the loan coming from just one person. I want you to find five people who'll lend you $2,500 each."

Immediately, I began phoning all the men I'd met at publishing parties who'd ever patted me on the back and said "Congratulations!" Within a week, I had my five, including the president of *Time* magazine. Tom was impressed. As I'd hoped, our summer issue was a huge success, and within six months, I'd paid all the investors back plus ten percent interest on their loans. My favorite thank-you note was from the chairman of Harlequin: "I was planning to return the $250 interest," he wrote, "but I know how much pride you have, so I want you to know that my wife and I went out and had a very good dinner!" I think I laughed out loud.

Soon we were making a steady profit and winning awards. When we came up with the idea of selling subscriptions as a retail product boxed with a free gift, our little upstart won a third-place bronze in the Canadian Marketing

Awards. For the first time in my life, I felt like I'd found my true purpose. Publishing used all my creative strengths, and I was writing a monthly column, as well, which was gaining an audience. An Air Canada service agent at the airport surprised me one day when she recognized the name on my ticket and asked for my autograph. She told me she read my columns faithfully.

OVER THE YEARS, Zan and I had remained in touch. Although I hadn't had the chance to return to Montreal after my Foufs adventure, Zan was busy rebuilding his business there and occasionally came to Toronto, where we'd catch up over lunch.

One day he called to say he'd received a major contract to design the interior of a luxury condominium in the city, and he wanted to meet me for lunch. He said he had something confidential to share and his voice was unusually subdued. At the end of the meal, he confided that he was HIV positive, swearing me to secrecy, worried if the news leaked out, the developers would fire him. He described the expensive, experimental drugs he was taking and told me he'd quit smoking, an enormous feat for a chain-smoker. I'd never seen him without a cigarette. "The fags!" he said, pounding the table with his fist. "If I can control only one fucking thing, it's gonna be those!" When he realized what he'd just said, he threw back his head and laughed. He never had trouble laughing at life's ironies; it was one of things I loved about him.

After we parted, I kept replaying his lunchtime confession in my head. He'd looked healthy enough, but I worried that it was only a matter of time. Whenever I spoke to him on the phone, he fretted about the precarious state of his finances and the expense of his drugs. Frantically, I began searching for news about experimental medical trials. We had a mutual friend in the pharmaceutical industry who I was sure might have leads, but Zan wouldn't let me ask him. I begged and begged but he was adamant, such was his fear of rejection and job loss. I wrestled with the moral dilemma of whether to honor his confidentiality. In the end, I decided it was his secret to keep; all I could do was offer support.

A year later, when the condominium was finally finished, he phoned to say he was flying in for the weekend to put the finishing touches on the model suite. The open house for prospective buyers was in three days' time. Could he stay with me?

I barely recognized him when he arrived at my door. He'd lost a staggering amount of weight. Weak and gaunt, he was dragging his overnight bag, barely making it over the threshold. In the living room, he collapsed on the sofa. I felt his forehead. He was burning up. Now he admitted he hadn't told me the whole truth: His HIV had progressed to AIDS, and in the middle of this job, which he desperately needed to fund his medication, he felt too exhausted to work. I looked at his wasted frame. How could he possibly decorate a model suite? He should be in hospital. Alarmed, I insisted he call the developer and cancel.

"Don't you understand?" he whispered. "Nobody can know! If anyone finds out, I'll lose the project. I need the money!" He began coughing, then grabbed my arm. "You do it," he begged, his voice raspy with fever. "Take my credit cards. Buy whatever you need."

"Me? Are you crazy? Look around you! You think I know anything about decorating?!"

"Tell them you're my assistant. Say I ordered everything. Say you're just installing it."

I looked at him in bewilderment. Had he not ordered anything? Where was this building? What did the space look like? What sort of things was I supposed to buy? Zan gave me the address. His instructions were brief. "Whatever you think," he said, and closed his eyes.

Immediately, the blind monk's voice flew into my head. *It's just theater,* it said calmly, *Nothing but a stage set.*

His words were oddly comforting. I knew nothing about decorating, but I did know how to stage a play. I drove to the site in a luxurious corner of the city and pictured the characters: wealthy, retired older couples. I pictured the props: fine antique furnishings. Over the next two days, I drove all over town like a madwoman on a rescue mission, feeling as pumped as any director before opening night. I bought everything from Persian carpets and fancy French linens to copper cookware and crystal towel racks, and had them all delivered to the sleek marble lobby of the condominium. The developer seemed a little surprised when I introduced myself, but there was so much confusion, with painters and plasterers colliding in a last-minute panic, that he didn't question me too closely. On the final day, I rushed over with vases of sweet-smelling flowers. I even bought an apple pie, popped it on a silver salver and threw it on the kitchen counter as though a maid would be back soon to finish serving dinner. The model suite was a huge success. I couldn't believe we pulled it off.

By Tuesday, Zan was too ill to fly. A friend drove him back to Montreal, where his health continued to deteriorate. Over the next two months, he phoned me constantly, fretting about money. His credit card charges had come due, and the developer hadn't paid him the final installment. After three months, he was desperate, convinced the developer had discovered he was deathly ill and was stalling, trying to run out the clock. I was incensed. Obviously, this play hadn't ended yet. There was a third act.

"Give me the developer's office address," I said angrily. "I'll get your check!"

Careful, said the blind monk, *you'll need the right costume for this one*.

Choosing my sexiest, most intimidating red suit and adding sparkling earrings, spike heels and a mink coat thrown casually over my shoulders, I drove to their offices and strode up to the receptionist like I owned the place. She waved at a closed mahogany door and told me the developer was in a meeting and couldn't be disturbed. I flounced right past her like I'd seen Katharine Hepburn do in the movies and flung open the door. The developer was sitting at the far end of a paneled room, behind his large leather-topped desk. A short chubby man sat across from him in a club chair, smoking a cigar and wearing alligator brogues.

"Excuse me, gentlemen, sorry to interrupt your meeting," I said, "but I'm here on urgent business." I looked down at the chubby man's feet and flashed him a flirtatious smile. "Nice shoes, by the way." He stumbled to stand up and shake my hand.

The developer remained seated, looking slightly amused, but his eyes began to narrow as if he were trying to place me; the first time he met me, I'd been dressed in jeans and a T-shirt.

"Sorry," he said, "but do I know you?"

"Yes. I'm Zan's assistant. We met at the open house three months ago. I'm here to pick up his check."

"Ah," he said, relaxing. "You want to speak to our accounts department. They take care of things like that."

"But they haven't taken care of it!" I said, deciding to cut to the quick. I'd kept Zan's secret for long enough. The time for secrets was over. "Let's be frank here. We both know Zan is dying. You're withholding the money he needs for his medication and I'm not leaving until you give it to me." As a kicker, I added, "You should be ashamed of yourself!"

The chubby man looked like he wanted to melt into the carpet. The developer scowled. But he opened his desk drawer, scrawled out a check for $18,000, leapt to his feet and ushered me out by the elbow, slamming the door behind me.

As soon as I got home, I jammed my fancy clothes back into my costume cupboard and called Zan. "Guess what?" I shouted over the phone. "I got your check!"

Tragically, it was all too late. Experimental drugs couldn't save him. He'd always told me he didn't want to die in a hospital, and I knew his God had no *d*, so it was sadly ironic when several months later, he ended up in a hospital called Hôtel-Dieu.

I flew to his bedside, bringing with me a few well-chosen flowers, the ones I knew he adored. Mounted on the wall outside his door was a box of rubber gloves to protect visitors. *Protect us from what*, I wondered, *from the life we share with Zan?* The worst had already happened. I'd followed him to the ends of his earth, and now all I could do was watch him go over the edge. I looked at the translucent blue fingertips dangling from the box and decided I wouldn't wear any. I wanted to feel his hands. Let him feel mine. Without taking any, I pushed my way in.

Inside the tiny room, Zan lay in a shallow metal crib. A single visitor's chair was jammed in the corner and his CD player sat on a shelf. His long arms and legs, once muscular and strong, were now wasted to thin, knobbly spindles. It seemed like only yesterday I was on the back of his motorbike, gripping his waist, zigzagging down hairpin turns on the black, tarred road to Lanzarote, hearing him shout, "Trust me!" I'd called him my Pied Piper then, a man who'd lured me away from my comfortable existence as a single mother with three young children, promising to inject adventure into my all-too-predictable life. With an immense zest for life, he'd always lived on the edge, daring others to join him. He was tall, rugged, handsome, with hypnotic eyes and a dazzling smile. Now his chestnut hair had fallen out in clumps. His teeth had fallen out, too, his lips collapsing inward. Only his eyes looked familiar, glowing like hot coals, feverish and bright, and they bulged when he saw me. I tucked the flowers in beside him, leaning close to his face. He pecked at me desperately, twisting his spine, one of his hands reaching for my neck, the other pulling his damp blue hospital gown up around his waist.

"My, my," said the nurse as she padded into the room to check his IV bag, "aren't we modest!" She pulled his gown back down. "You have more visitors waiting at the end of the hall." She rolled her eyes at me and whispered, "Don't stay too long."

As soon as she swooshed out the door, Zan pointed to the picture of the Virgin Mary hanging opposite his bed and muttered, "*Cover* that thing!"

I grabbed a flimsy white washcloth from the foot of his bed and slung it over her. "How's that? Better?" Then I reached over and clicked on his CD player. Immediately, the voice of Teresa Stratas filled the room with the soaring final duet from *La Bohème*.

Without ever taking his eyes from my face, Zan began plucking blooms from the bouquet I'd laid by his side. He stuck the bird-of-paradise inside his left ear, its prickly hot-pink and lime-green tail feathers fanning out across the white pillow beside his cheek. He poked the stem of the orange lily inside his right nostril so that its blossom splayed across his upper lip and the edges of its petals fluttered faintly as he breathed. And finally, with a grimace (or was it a smile?), he wedged the purple freesia alongside the catheter tube that snaked through the railing and over the edge of the bed. It seemed to me this was his last artistic act; he'd transformed his useless body—the one he could no longer control, the one that had let him down—into a vase.

There was a time when I had thought I alone belonged to Zan, but now I met his other lovers in the visitors' room at the end of the hall. His former wife, whom he'd married in his twenties when she was a much older woman, was perched on the edge of a brown leatherette chair. She was dressed in a long, black coat and was leaning on a cane, her wispy, gray hair tucked up in a bun, a silk scarf pinned tidily at her throat with a brooch. She held out a gloved hand and mumbled "bonjour" when I introduced myself, then cast her hooded eyes back to the floor.

Zan's current girlfriend was standing by the window, watching young pigeons strutting outside on the gritty flat roof. She was a graduate student in her early thirties, dressed in a black leather miniskirt, her pretty heart-shaped face framed by waist-length brown hair.

A tall, handsome lawyer in his early forties with two days of stubble, who I assumed was Zan's boyfriend, was dressed in a brown suede blazer and blue jeans. He'd brought his five-year-old son with him.

And then, of course, there was me.

We studied each other with curiosity and made awkward small talk, knowing we were all important to Zan, but unsure where each of us fit. Obviously, we'd all been his "secret-keepers" and were still in the thrall of this man, a tortured, evolving soul who'd meant so many different things to each of us.

Eventually, we stopped taking turns to visit and crowded into his room together, surrounding his bed. Zan mumbled something about wanting to spend a final night with me in my hotel room, but we all knew he was delirious. "Dream on!" I said, and everyone laughed.

He died a few days later. I like to imagine that he left in a haze of morphia just as Teresa Stratas hit a high note, but I wasn't there. I'd taken the train back home, already grieving the loss of my soulmate.

He had often described his life as like being stretched on a rack and sliced into sections and wanting to die from the agony. It made me think about bodies transforming. Why are some of us punished for the bodies our souls are born into, especially if souls are used over and over again, as I often pondered in childhood?

I thought of all that Zan had been forced to repress in his life, spanning as it did an era when same-sex activity between consenting adults was reviled, sometimes even criminalized; when many didn't dare admit they were gay or bisexual, especially if they wanted a family with children. I thought of the vilification they'd all suffered for a virus that wasn't their fault, yet it had picked them off, one by one. I wondered if any of his young Spanish friends were still alive, the ones in Las Palmas who'd stood guard with machine guns slung over their shoulders, watching for unseen enemies in the dark, as if their guns could save them. And I thought of Dr. Pavillard, who may have saved my life.

I WENT HOME TO MY CHILDREN, my work and Simon. For five years, my relationship with Simon had been supportive and rewarding, but despite our best efforts, things weren't working out. Our timing was off. Just as Simon's children were reaching adulthood and the demands on his time were decreasing, demands on my time were increasing.

My children were entering their teenage years and no longer wanted to spend weekends at the farm. Simon was going without me. In the city, he wanted more of my time, but I seemed to have less and less of it. He wanted to travel, but I couldn't take time off from work. The strain was too much on our relationship. One night, Simon admitted that he'd met someone new, and I didn't know what to do with his honest confession. "Please don't cry," he said, but I couldn't help it. I cried into his shoulder, blaming myself. It felt like just as my work life was blossoming, my personal life had died. Why couldn't I have it all?

It was spring 1989, and the very next day, I was driving my children to the Hershey's Chocolate World in Pennsylvania for their March Break holiday. While they sat in the back seat, each plugged into their own Sony Walkman listening to music, tears streamed down my face, and that night, after the children were asleep, I sobbed in the motel bathroom. The toilet had a reddish-brown rust stain at the bottom of its bowl that reminded me of blood after a murder scene. It took me most of that year to get over Simon. He had been part of my Rapunzel story, but I'd been too preoccupied with my own creative ambition to see it.

I decided I didn't know how to love, not consistently, not past the seven-year itch, not till death do us part. I had no idea why. Lord knows, I'd had enough practice. Perhaps I'd made wrong choices or failed to understand men or, most probably, failed to understand myself. Perhaps I'd had lousy role models. Possibly, I was too selfish, too independent, too opinionated to be a good partner. I'd never been a good team player. I liked my own space. On the other hand, if my friend Pat was right and you only get to know yourself through relationships, perhaps I had so many different sides to myself that I needed many men to explore them all.

I searched for clues in dozens of books with titles like *Women Who Love Too Much*, *Please Understand Me*, *The Dance of Anger* and *Codependent No More*. In fact, a few months after my failed relationship with Simon, I found I had amassed an entire library on the subject and happily hoisted the whole collection—bookshelf and all—out to the sidewalk for our next garage sale. Feeling a tad embarrassed by what neighbors might deduce from my reading material, I was relieved when a stranger soon bought the whole kit and caboodle. He seemed nervous. As he rushed it into the trunk of his car, I didn't have the heart to tell him that the most important title—*Love for Dummies*—was missing. Apparently, nobody had written it yet. There was *Sex for Dummies*, *Flirting for Dummies*, *Dating for Dummies*, even *Happiness for Dummies*. But love? It wasn't in the Dummies lineup. Perhaps it's not teachable. Perhaps it's the only thing we must learn for ourselves. The trouble is, so few of us learn.

Bluebeard

OF COURSE, I TURNED OUT to be the biggest dummy of all. I'd no sooner sold all the books and sworn off men forever than I was swept off my feet by a charismatic widower with a brood of young children. It turned out that I had many more lessons to learn about what love is . . . and what it isn't.

I wasn't going to tell you this story because the material is so toxic that when I try to remember, my body starts to shake just like it did thirty-five years ago whenever I drove down his street. I'm an old woman now and most of my friends have a story like mine. When we gather, it's often our topic of conversation—this *waste of our years*. How? Why?

Charles Perrault first recorded the story of Bluebeard in the seventeenth century, yet *nothing has changed*. Women from all over the world continue to walk into this trap.

In the story of Bluebeard, a powerful, wealthy man goes shopping for a wife. Under false pretenses, he manages to lure a beautiful young maiden by appearing generous and kind. He lavishes her with attention and promises to give her the keys to his castle. She decides to overlook his ugly blue beard and the fact that he has been married many times before, and she accepts his proposal of marriage. Immediately after the wedding, he leaves on a trip and tells her she may use any key she likes to unlock rooms of riches, but she's forbidden to use the tiny key to the room at the end of the passage. Of course, her curiosity is piqued. After she delights in the riches of the other rooms, she unlocks the last door and finds the nightmare of his true nature: The bodies of all his dead wives line the walls, and the floor is awash in blood.

I'm still furious that I got sucked in, that I wasted so many of my best years. I should feel relief, even pride—after all, I escaped—but I needed to sift through mountains of broken memories to understand how I became ensnared in the first place and, more importantly, *why I stayed*.

I'd just turned forty-two, an attractive, intelligent woman at the height of my career, financially secure, in love with life, successfully raising three children of my own as a single parent, and he was a delusion, a projection of my own fantasy.

I created him in an instant, the moment we met, when through the window of a school after a parent-teacher meeting, I saw him outside pacing back and forth trying to find the courage (so he said) to ask me out on a date. I'd already heard from other parents the sad story of how his wife had been killed in a car crash, leaving him alone and bereft with small children to raise. His circumstance tugged at my heart and created a space for him to enter. He looked like the man next door, and everything about him plugged into the family fairy tale I'd been dragging behind me since childhood. Finally, I could reenact the rescue of Dad. I could step right into that small silver-framed photo of Miss Alice, the one that Dad always kept on his dresser, and become the woman he worshipped, the woman who'd sacrificed her life to raise a bunch of motherless children. Somewhere, deep in my subconscious, I'd always wanted to be her. Of course, I wasn't that insightful at the time.

The chemistry between us was instant, the attraction so fierce and powerful, it felt like the force of an undertow. Bouquets of flowers began arriving at my office. He lavished his attention, taking me out to lunches and dinners and calling me multiple times a day, just quick calls to say he was missing me. Within weeks, he had introduced me to his small children, who clung to me. I was entranced by his boyish enthusiasm, his intense *neediness*, the way he lusted after me, grabbed for me, devoured me, and by the time the summer was over, there was no turning back: It was as if I'd been cast under a spell. He told me he'd never imagined he could have a woman like me, that I was the love of his life; he wanted to carry me away, have me all to himself, for us to "become one."

I overlooked the fact that we had nothing in common— why break the spell? His housekeeper had quit, his household was in complete disarray, and he needed me. I wanted to be needed, so when he began asking me to run errands or to care for his children when he had an important business trip to attend, I was happy to fit it into my own busy schedule. Soon, I was canceling my own events to give priority to his . . . and gradually, his needs overcame mine. The seduction of those early days slowly began to change. Soon he had heaped on so many demands that I could barely think straight, but I was too exhausted to notice.

When he murmured sweetly that he wanted me all to himself, I didn't recognize the beginning of a jealous possessiveness. He complained that my mother called too often. He didn't like me speaking to the neighbors. He didn't like my friends. Small put-downs crept into his language, initially couched as jokes; when they became cruel, and I reacted in tears, his response was why was I so sensitive? Where was my sense of humor? He began criticizing the way I walked, the way I styled my hair, the clothes I wore. He trivialized my work and said my business took up too much of my time. He wanted me to sell my company. The adage of the frog sitting in a pot of water perfectly describes what was happening to me: As he gradually turned up the heat, I acclimatized and didn't realize how hot the water was getting.

As time went on, things came to a boil. His moods would swing wildly for no apparent reason. He started blaming me for anything that went wrong; I was always the cause: If only I hadn't raised my voice . . . or left when I did . . . or burnt his toast . . . or made him late. I spent my time and energy trying to figure out what I was doing wrong, and how I could do better, but his demands were so unpredictable. I was always in a state of confusion, trying to make sense out of nonsense. Was he still grieving his wife? Was he drinking too much? Did he have some kind of personality disorder?

He kept saying, "I'll never let you go, my love, and therein lies the key."

My relationship with Bluebeard lasted almost ten years—seven years fully in it, and a further three years as I went back and forth "in rehearsal," as one therapist put it, trying to escape. The water had become so deep and dangerous that by the time it was over, I'd almost completely submerged my personality.

One afternoon, my son Carter arrived home unexpectedly from college. He found me curled up in the fetal position on our kitchen floor, crying.

"Mom! Mom!" he shouted with alarm. "Mom! What's wrong?!" I found I couldn't hold it in anymore. I had wanted to protect my children from it, but it was too late. I was a madwoman.

"Carter, I smell!" I cried. "I smell bad! I smell bad everywhere! My arms, my hair, my breath, everywhere!"

"What are you talking about?"

"I do, I do. He says I smell bad. Everything about me smells bad!" I wept and rocked and held my sides together as if my guts would spill out onto the linoleum.

"Oh my God, Mom!" He leaned down to hold me and hug me. As he was holding me, he said gently, "You don't smell bad, you know. You don't!"

I remember catching my breath. It was as though I was hearing his distant voice coming from a faraway place, a place where sane people lived. His voice brought me back.

"I don't?" I gulped for air.

"No, you don't!"

"You mean it? You're not just saying that?" I was still sobbing. My hair was wet from tears and plastered to my forehead.

"Mom!" he said, more forcefully now. "You smell good!" And then a look of disgust crossed his face. "I can't believe he does this to you! I can't believe you let him! Can't you see what he's doing? How he makes you feel so bad about yourself? You do everything for him, and he just puts you down. It's evil!"

I felt so ashamed that Carter had found me like this. "But he doesn't mean to," I said, weeping. "He loves me!"

"That's not love, Mom. Can't you see that? No one treats somebody they love like this! You're the most wonderful person. You have so many friends. They all love you. Do any of them treat you like this?"

After Carter cleaned me up, I went to the dining room table and laid out a huge piece of paper. Taking colored markers, I tried to document my pain. I couldn't articulate it, the words froze in my brain, but the raw colors bled from my markers. I titled the page *Where Insecurities Come From.*

Art had always helped me make sense of the world, so I began using it as an act of survival, my anchor to reality. Over the following years, whenever events happened that were beyond my understanding, I sketched them, hoping that if I looked at them later, they would make sense to me. But nothing ever made sense, because I was trying to make sense out of nonsense, and eventually I stored my sketches in a box in the attic.

I SPENT MY TIME STUDYING books about grieving, alcoholism and narcissistic personality disorders. There seemed to be a demon inside him, hell-bent on destroying the very love he claimed he so desperately wanted, so I went to doctors, therapists and Al-Anon meetings. I kept trying to fix him, instead of fixing *myself.*

Whenever I found the strength to leave him, he'd woo me back with tearful apologies and promises of change that were as intense as his anger. It had all the sinister earmarks of addiction, because it was seductive to feel I could, with one last throw of the dice, win back everything I'd invested. By then I'd invested everything, down to the very core of my being. Eventually, it felt impossible to get out because I'd exhausted myself. I'd lost my will to leave. I'd stopped trusting my own perceptions and was in deep psychological shock. A kind of amnesia set in, where I literally forgot abusive episodes in order to live with myself. I stopped telling friends and family what was really going on, because how could I rationalize staying if they knew? I didn't want to lose him—I just wanted him to get better! The cycle of abuse escalated and became so repetitive that each time I adapted. But that's when my body started to shake whenever I drove down his street.

My Bluebeard's favorite expression was "Perception is reality!" He would shout it exuberantly whenever he tried to impress others by buying an expensive suit, or an extravagant sports car, or VIP box seats for a baseball game. "Perception is reality!" But I was always thinking, *Perception is never reality, except to those you're trying to fool.* Reality is reality—and one day, it rears up and smacks you in the face. If you're lucky.

One night, I finally decided to face the truth. I'd known it for years, of course, but it had been too painful to acknowledge; I'd been lying to myself—just like he had.

Like Bluebeard's wife, I used a tiny key. I unlocked the trunk in his closet that he claimed contained his dead wife's mementoes, and there I discovered the evidence—cards, letters, photographs—of fourteen other women, all of whom he'd been seducing during our years together. *Fourteen!* Imagine his balancing act. They included flight attendants, secretaries, teachers, nannies, executives and mothers like me. It was just like when Bluebeard's new wife unlocked a secret chamber and found the corpses of all his previous wives.

It's hard to describe the effect of confirming that your reality never existed. It's as if a bomb explodes in your brain.

Every memory fragments. You have no coherent past. If someone says to you, "What happened next?" you can't remember. Your life lies in ashes on the floor, the translucent gray bits floating in the air, impossible to read, or grasp, or make whole and string together. How can you possibly testify? Your memory is full of holes, like Swiss cheese. You might get triggered, might suddenly have a flashback lying in bed late at night, but daylight comes, and you stumble and weep and can't get back there because you have become an unreliable witness to your own life. Eventually, I managed to meet some of the other women. Several had received marriage proposals. Some thought I was the nanny. But the only solid truth I have of those years are the sketches I made in real time.

BLUEBEARD WAS AWAY ON A business trip to Japan when I told him over the phone what I'd found in the trunk. He denied it, said I was misinterpreting things, he would explain later, and I still wanted to believe him, still wanted to avoid the pain of reality. I was still willing to give it one last chance.

He arrived home at midnight by limousine and bounded up to the bedroom. Before I could raise my head, he dove on top of me and smothered my face with kisses. "I've missed you so much," he said. "Every waking minute . . . you'll never know how much I've missed you!" He hauled his two heavy suitcases onto the bed, squishing my feet with their weight.

"I bought you so many beautiful things!" He rummaged through his cases to find them. "Stand up, close your eyes." He made me get out of bed and stand with my eyes closed and my arms outstretched. I felt something soft and smooth drape over my arms.

"Ready?" He laughed. "Okay, open!"

I looked down. A long, white silk kimono hung on my body, the hem shimmering with gold embroidery.

"That's not all," he whispered playfully. "Close your eyes again!" I heard the rustle of tissue. He slipped the first one off me and slipped on another. I opened my eyes. Another kimono, this one bright orange.

"Another one?" I said, testing the water. "Who's this one for?"

"I couldn't decide which color, so I thought, shit, buy her both!" He swept me into his arms. "Do you like them? Really?"

I didn't know what to say, so I said nothing. I could feel myself sliding back into denial.

"I just felt so passionately about you!" he whispered. "Everywhere I went, I saw you. There's never a second goes by when I don't think of you. I could hardly wait to get home, to be with you, to hold you like this." He lifted my face to his and kissed me softly. "I want it always to be like this. Please don't throw us away. I know you've had a hard time with the children while I've been away, but I'm home now. Everything will be okay. Trust me, lover."

I felt his tongue travel down the side of my neck as he brushed my hair to one side. Then he lifted me up and laid me gently on the bed. The sheets were still warm from my earlier sleep. "I'd give you anything to make you happy," he murmured as he kissed me. "Anything. You know that." In a haze of loving slow motion, I felt hope once again seeping into my soul. "Say you'll be mine," he whispered. "Say you'll be mine—forever!"

We awoke early in the same position sleep found us, completely intertwined. My face was nestled in his neck, my belly curled into his, one of his legs thrown over my hips. Our eyes fluttered open simultaneously. He touched my face gently and traced the side of my cheek. "I don't think I'm ever going to admire anyone the way I admire you."

When we got out of bed, we surveyed the disarray of his bags, half unpacked. "Wait a minute," Bluebeard said, rummaging around the second bag, "I saved the best for the last!"

"More?" I laughed.

He quickly whipped something behind his back. "Which hand?"

"Both!"

With a grin, he held out a padded evening jacket, the heavy yellow silk printed with white cranes soaring towards blue clouds. The early morning light reflected off the silver threads outlining the clouds and sent circles of sunny dots dancing on the walls. "I couldn't resist!" he said. "There were so many beautiful things in the shop, and they all reminded me of you." I slipped it on and twirled at my reflection in the gilt-edged mirror. "I want you to wear it the very next time we go out for dinner. Promise? In fact, you can pack it when we go to Antigua for your birthday next month!"

I laughed to myself. It would be far too hot to wear in Antigua, but I loved his delight in his purchase; he was trying so hard to please me. Shouldn't I make the other women a distant memory? They were "in the past," just as he'd said, and I should leave them there. If he'd made mistakes, his love for me now was stronger than ever.

IN NOVEMBER, WE FLEW to Antigua. It was even hotter than usual. A hurricane had recently passed through like a vacuum, sucking away all the cooling breezes. Bluebeard hated it, spending most days sleeping in our air-conditioned room. The thoughtful, adoring lover I'd welcomed back only three weeks earlier had disappeared. Over dinner in the evenings, he barely spoke to me.

On my birthday morning, I awoke early with excited anticipation. The sun was already streaming through the shutters. Virginia had tucked a book and card into my suitcase, so I tiptoed into the bathroom to unwrap it. Leaving Bluebeard to sleep, I changed into my bikini and wandered up the path to the hotel pool to swim some lengths before breakfast. I was the only swimmer, but under the gazebo at the far end, a few male lawyers in Bermuda shorts and loafers were holding a seminar, gathering early before the heat worsened, the sun already beating down on the empty deck chairs around them. I imagined their wives still sleeping peacefully in their air-conditioned rooms, like Bluebeard.

As I began my solitary laps, the sky filled with an infestation of tiny pastel butterflies that fluttered above me as I swam, rising and falling like handfuls of yellow, pink and blue confetti. I swam the breaststroke gracefully, gliding between strokes with my childhood swim coach's voice in my ear, stretching my body taut, head down, fingers straight. ("Glide further! Make those heel tips break the water! Perfect! Perfect!")

The audience of lawyers had their backs to me, but the speaker could see me well, and I smiled into the water whenever he stuttered or lost his train of thought. His voice carried across the water, and every time I came up for air, I caught snatches of corporate law in a Southern accent. For a while, I felt weightless, lost in concentration, and then I heard her.

"Gee-awge!" she drawled as she sauntered across the patio towards the speaker, her mules click-clacking on the flagstone. "D'yall have a room key, hon?" She was rummaging through her beach bag. "I'm goin' for a walk by the beach." Her blonde pageboy framed an aging face, pearl earrings bobbing under a large straw hat, and she was squinting into the sun in my direction. A gossamer shift covered her bathing suit.

I knew her husband's craggy, dignified face better than I knew hers, but until this moment, I hadn't put these two people together as a couple. Her husband didn't seem to mind the interruption to his speech. He simply smiled in her direction, reached into his pocket and held up his room key to reassure her. I remember thinking how polite he was. Was that the easy kind of relationship most couples had?

I lifted myself up by the side of the pool, water streaming from my bikini, hair and fingertips, and toweled off. I could see Bluebeard walking up the pathway.

"Where have you been?" he snarled.

"Doing my lengths."

"I've been waiting for you!" He stalked off towards the outdoor breakfast buffet.

I went back to our room and hurriedly changed. At breakfast, I found him already seated, eating eggs and bacon. "I didn't know what you wanted," he said, without looking up.

I went to the buffet and got a croissant and a glass of grapefruit juice. Before I even sat down, he took my juice and drank it. "Get me another," he said, burping and holding up the empty glass, "but make it a large one, this time."

"Who was your servant last year?" I joked.

"You," he said without smiling, "and the service was just as bad."

I hesitated a moment. Should I make an issue of this? His mood was ugly. It felt like my birthday was about to be sabotaged, and I didn't want to give him any unnecessary ammunition. I got his juice. We ate in silence.

As we were finishing, I noticed that the speaker's wife from my morning swim had returned from her stroll along the beach and was sitting just two tables away. She was waiting for coffee, but the staff had disappeared.

In exasperation, she called out, "Is there any service 'round here?" No one came. She said a little louder, "Could I please have some coffee?"

I leaned over to Bluebeard and said softly, "Why don't you take our coffee pot and offer her some of ours."

"I will not!" he said through clenched teeth, glaring at me. "Why can't you ever, *just once*, mind your own fucking business!" I started to get up to do it myself, but he grabbed my wrist. "Don't you dare think about doing it either!"

I stared at him. Something deep within my personality demanded to survive. I thought, *I will be who I am. This man will not stop me from being who I am!*

Very slowly, I got up. Dramatically draping my white linen serviette over my arm like a waiter, I lifted our silver coffee pot up with a flourish and glided over to her table. "Please," I said, "allow me."

"O-ooh," she squealed, "aren't you *wunnerful*!" She giggled. "You saved my life!"

When I turned back to our table, Bluebeard was already angrily throwing his crumpled serviette onto his chair and walking past me in disgust.

The punishment he chose for my birthday was the silent treatment. All day. I received no present, no card, no cake, no kiss, nothing. I thought of my darling children and Mum and Dad, all of whom would have given anything to be with me. I knew they were thinking of me. At the end of the day,

Bluebeard said, "Remember that jacket I brought you from Tokyo? That was your birthday present."

I lay awake for hours that night, trying to understand why I stayed with a man whose behavior I abhorred. My own children, mercifully, were all away at school, but how could I be with a man I didn't even want them exposed to? What was I doing?

WE'RE LED TO BELIEVE THAT Bluebeard's story ends when his young wife's brothers ride to her rescue, killing Bluebeard before he kills her. And most people might think that when Bluebeard attacked me, it was the end of my story. But they would be wrong.

In my memory, the real finale came a little earlier, the night he invited me to bring Dad for dinner. Mum was away that weekend and I was looking after Dad. Alzheimer's had robbed Dad of almost everything by then. He couldn't string a sentence together and rarely spoke; he simply stared into space.

We arrived at Bluebeard's castle only to find there was no dinner; I was expected to cook. Bluebeard sat down at his dining room table, sloshing his wine, and began to tell Dad off-color jokes. He shouted to me in the kitchen, "Hurry up in there, fatso! And bring me more wine!" When I brought in the food, he said, "Who cooked this shit?" When I tried to make polite conversation, he shrugged and wouldn't answer me. We'd only eaten a few mouthfuls when Bluebeard burped and said, "Why don't you leave now. I think your father would rather be sitting on his porch—wouldn't you, old man?"

"What a good idea!" I said brightly, swallowing my disgust, not wanting Dad to suffer one more indignity. I rushed to his side, helped him to the car, buckled him in and started the engine. I turned to look at Dad's face. It was expressionless. Bluebeard stood looming in front of the car with his hands on his hips.

"Does he always treat you this badly?" said Dad. He was staring straight ahead, and it was the first thoughtful sentence I'd heard him utter in months. I knew then that the truth I'd been denying was obvious even to someone with Alzheimer's.

I finally accepted that the man I loved didn't exist, except in my own longing.

Through the Dark Woods

THE BLUEBEARD YEARS had taken their toll. During those years, my brother Sandy died of cancer, Dad required a triple bypass, Mum had a stroke and then Dad was diagnosed with Alzheimer's.

Eventually, I buckled under the strain of trying to run a business while raising children, caring for Mum and Dad and dealing with Bluebeard. I decided to sell my company. It took several years to find the right buyer, one that would agree to keep my loyal employees on the payroll, but finally, in 1993, we sold to Torstar. My accountant congratulated me and said if I was "careful," I'd never have to work again.

But I wasn't careful. I couldn't escape my entrepreneurial nature. Over the next several years, I cofounded *Help's Here*, a magazine for caregivers and then, in 1996, I invented the Pictureball, a Christmas ornament designed to hold photographs. But none of my projects provided much income, and by 2001, I'd lost most of the financial independence I'd gained by selling my publishing company. I had finally escaped Bluebeard but, distracted by all the upheaval in my personal life, I hadn't been paying attention. My investments began to collapse in a freefall with the burst of the telecom bubble, and I had difficulty paying my mortgage. It felt like I'd lost everything I'd worked for in the past twenty years, and all my dreams for the future. How could I have been so impulsive? And why couldn't I answer the question that had plagued me since my first day at nursery school: Who was I?

THE FOLLOWING SPRING, my brother Chris flew to Toronto for a visit. For years, he'd been living in Saskatoon, where he was president of St. Andrew's Theological College, and we rarely had time alone together without family around us. We were sitting in a restaurant, racing to catch up over lunch, filling each other in on the personal details of our lives. As I tried to explain what had happened during the last years of my relationship with Bluebeard, I noticed beads of moisture trickling down the side of his face.

"Why are you sweating?" I asked. "Too hot?"

"It's not the heat," he said, looking up from his plate, "it's the story I'm hearing."

Later, as I was driving him back to his hotel, he said, "Have you written all this down, your thoughts, your feelings?"

"No."

"Why not?"

"Because it's too awful, too sordid. Who would want to read it? It's like something from a TV talk show."

Chris turned to look at me. "Why do you think this sort of stuff is on talk shows in the first place? It's because it's important. It's what people need to know!"

I knew I could never write about it. My shame was too great. But later that day when I returned home, I went up to the attic on the third floor and opened my box of sketches. All the pain and anger came rushing back—anger at *myself* for allowing it. I felt sick to my stomach. My mind could rationalize and deny, but my art was irrefutable. It was like looking at old video footage from my own bodycam. Maybe my art had been sufficient. I'd survived. And now maybe I could use those feelings to force the rage out of my throat. I decided to share my sketches with Chris.

The next day, I stuffed them into a fat manila envelope, threw them into my bicycle basket and rode over to my local copy shop a few blocks away to make some copies. Inside the shop, brawny young men with tattoos on their arms and bandannas tied across their foreheads were operating

machinery in the back. Posters of Grand Prix races decorated the walls, and I imagined they all rode motorcycles to
work and tinkered with car engines on weekends. I wondered
what their real dreams were as they stacked heavy cardstock
and repetitively operated the hole punchers. As I waited my
turn at the front counter, they bantered back and forth with
off-color jokes.

"How many copies?" barked Tony as I handed him my
envelope.

"Just one each, please. Can you do it while I wait?" I
was afraid to let them out of my sight.

"Sure thing!" He glanced up at the wall clock. "How
'bout ten minutes?"

Removing my sketches from the envelope, he handed
them to Joe, who was standing next to the photocopier. Joe
began turning them face down, but I noticed that he'd
slowed down to pay attention. He nudged another sidekick,
who turned to look. Soon, Tony joined them. I strained to
see which one had grabbed their attention. It portrayed a
drunken Bluebeard screaming at me.

When the job was finished, Tony brought the pages back
to the counter. "So," he said, "were these done by . . . like . . .
a kid?"

"No," I said, too embarrassed to admit they were mine.
"An artist friend of mine did them."

"No kidding?" He looked at me curiously, as if he'd seen
through my disguise. I'd been using this copy shop for years

and knew Tony by name, but I'd never had a personal conversation with him. Brushing invisible dirt off the counter with his hands, he leaned forward and lowered his voice. "Y'know, my old man is buried in Mount Pleasant Cemetery, just around the corner."

"He is?"

"Yep. I pass by every day on my way to work, but to this day, I've never gone in."

"How come?"

"People say I should, but for what?" He punched his fist on the counter. "I hated him when he was alive, and I hated him after he died! He's exactly where he should be."

I was stunned. How did one of my sketches elicit this sudden outburst? Tony had always been so warm and generous, his desk proudly lined with photos of his wife and toddlers. Obviously, his upbeat nature hid deep scars from childhood.

"What do I owe you?" I asked, as he stacked my photocopies into a box.

"Nothing," he said. "And good luck to you!"

THAT NIGHT I HAD A NIGHTMARE.

Suddenly, in the middle of the night, headlights from Bluebeard's black Ferrari illuminated my bedroom like two searing searchlights. I heard a car door slam and boots running up our outdoor steps. *Bam-bam-bam!* Neptune's brass knocker crashed against the door and the whole house shook, the walls vibrating all the way up to the third floor. As I raced to peer over the banister, I saw that Bluebeard had slammed one of my sketches—the one the copy shop boys had been staring at—dog-eared and strangled, up against the window of the front door. "Is this yours?!" he screamed. "Is this yours?!" *POW!* He punched his beefy arm, fist-first, right through the glass. Shards exploded into my front hall. Blood spurted everywhere—not my blood, but his—and suddenly I sat up, wide awake. My heart was pounding.

As I shook myself from the dream, I thought, *I must do something about that window—put up a curtain, or something.*

THE NEXT DAY, I WENT to visit my friend Pat. As usual, her front door was unlocked, so when I knocked and got no answer, I let myself in and followed the sound of her pneumatic drill to the tiny studio at the back of her house, where she was carving a new piece of stone. On the wall behind her, I could see a faded piece of paper tacked to her bulletin board on which she'd copied down her favorite quotes from artists, poets, philosophers and saints.

"How lovely!" she said when she saw me. She put down her tools and took a moment to put her hearing aids back in. "How are you?"

"I'm in a turmoil, Pat." I gave her a hug. "I've been having so many bad dreams recently."

"Oh dear . . . let's make tea and you can tell me all about it."

She went into the kitchen, while I continued into her living room. It was awash in sunlight. For decades, she'd taught art at the National Ballet School, but none of her own paintings hung on the walls. Instead, she'd hung portraits by her late husband and large abstracts painted by her daughter.

"When did you stop painting, Pat?" I asked her.

"I was seventy-seven, dear! I had a dream that told me I needed to put down my brush and take up stone carving."

"But wasn't that hard?"

"Hard as hell." She laughed. "But that didn't stop me! Before stone, I was doing things that sold well, like my flower paintings. I sold hundreds of them. But working with stone is different. Stone breaks just at the point when you think you have it right, and then you must start from scratch again! It's a very different level of working. In that respect, it's like life."

"That's exactly how I feel," I said. "My life feels broken, and I don't know how to put the pieces back together again."

"Why would you want to save the bits that have scattered around your feet? They've already served their purpose. By falling away, they're giving you clarity!"

"No, they're not. They're giving me nightmares! Nothing in my life makes sense anymore."

"Maybe you need to try a different medium! You're obviously working through something. Sometimes in life, we're required to accept *subtraction*. Especially as we get older. In very old age, like me, it's the gradual loss of everything we previously took for granted—eyesight, hearing, muscle, mobility . . . even our hair, for goodness' sake. When our physical bodies lose shape, we shift our focus away from the physical world and more towards our spiritual interior. It's about *deconstruction*. Focusing less on detail and more on finding the *essential*. In other words, dear . . . *abstraction*!"

"But I've reinvented myself so many times, jumping from job to job, project to project and even relationship to relationship. I don't even know who I am anymore."

"You're *you*." She laughed. "Although you've got bigger and older, the essence of who you were when you began is still there. I'm still the same rebel I was as a little thing. Even in my nineties, I'm *still* trying to be me! As Richard Bach talked about in his book *One*, we're each given a block of stone when we begin a life, and the tools to shape it. You can drag it behind you untouched . . . you can pound it into gravel . . . or you can shape it into glory. The same thing goes for pain! You can leave it unexamined, or you can turn it into something beautiful!" She turned and began walking away. "Come," she said, "I want to show you something."

I followed her into her living room, where sheets of multicolored tissue paper lay on her glass-topped table. "I've been experimenting," she said. "It's quite a delightful exercise." Handing me a piece of cardboard and a bottle of white glue, she told me to choose my favorite tissue paper colors, rip them into small random shapes without thinking or caring and then glue them onto the cardboard in layers, abstractly. She left me there and disappeared back into her studio. The pieces were fragile, like working with a mosaic of feathers, but where colors overlapped, they produced new colors, and newer layers supplanted older ones. The glue was drying transparently, creating a sheen like a stained glass window. When she reappeared sometime later, I'd been so absorbed in my work, I didn't notice that an hour had gone by. "You've created new beauty, I see!" she said.

Before I left, she invited me to join her in a group show at the Women's Art Association called Imaging the Self. It was such a loaded title for me, but I knew I needed to confront myself once and for all. I'd recently painted a self-portrait, so I knew I could exhibit that, but what else could I make that would coax my "self" into being? And what new mediums could I use, as Pat had suggested?

I went down to my basement, letting the anger and paranoid fear from my dreams fuel my creativity. Subconscious thoughts bubbled up. I began soaking yesterday's news in the laundry tub, pounding the pulp to a porridge until my fists were gray from the ink and the tips of my fingers were puckered like prunes. I had no idea what I was making until, intuitively, the papier-mâché began shaping itself into oversized paper plates and bowls. Once they were dry, I found myself decorating them with painted images of my disconnected body parts, as if they were domestic canvases from a landfill of family picnics. I gave them playful titles like *Breastplate*, *Faceplate* and *Finger Bowl*, but their message was obvious—as a woman, I'd never felt so disposable.

Children were uppermost on my mind at that time. I was suffering enormous guilt for having taken time away from my own children's needs to deal with the crises presented by Bluebeard's family and sadness that I'd been forbidden to see his children after our relationship ended, so when a local murder trial was broadcast on television, I found myself creating another piece of art: *The Sampler Child*.

Years earlier, five-year-old Farah Khan's body parts had been found in garbage bags along the Toronto waterfront and now, finally, her parents were being brought to justice. Initially, nobody knew who the body parts belonged to, but Farah's kindergarten teacher had saved one of her finger paintings, and when it was given to the police, her fingerprints solved the mystery. I was consumed with the idea that Farah—like all artists—had left her mark. She'd identified herself through her art.

I knew that throughout history, young girls had often left their mark by embroidering "samplers." Using colored silk thread on pieces of linen, they carefully cross-stitched their name and birth date, along with the tiny letters of the alphabet in a variety of stitches. So I began to make one for Farah. In the evenings, as I sat glued to the televised trial of her father and stepmother, I felt like Madame Dufarge from *A Tale of Two Cities*—stitching and watching. Thinking of Farah's birth mother back in Pakistan, I cross-stitched a protective circle of Muslim mothers around the perimeter. Then, as more and more gruesome details emerged,

I cross-stitched the words *I am screaming* across an apartment building embroidered with flames. I punctuated the numerals 911 with images of tiny green garbage bags, and then I cross-stitched the alphabet. Much to my surprise, the letters N O appeared dead center, so I threaded some of my own hair through her O as a final memento mori.

I fantasized about groups of women sitting down to embroider samplers for all the murdered children in Canada, touring the collection across the country like Judy Chicago had done with her installation *The Dinner Party*. At the Women's Art Association exhibit, I stuck a note on the wall, asking anyone who was interested to contact me, but nobody did. In fact, most people recoiled. Wandering through the crowd on opening night, I overheard one man mutter, "Christ, there're a lot of angry women in here!" But he was staring at *The Sampler Child*, and there was only one angry woman standing behind him—me.

I did sell one piece that night: my self-portrait titled *She's a Real Dish!* Although it was humorous, it was full of dark undercurrents. I'd hauled a large canvas in front of the mirrored wall in my kitchen and painted myself sitting atop the stove. I was wearing an apron, but visible underneath was my tight leopard-print skirt, hot-pink camisole and red high heels. I was determined to be all things: artist, mother, woman, me. If you looked closely, you'd notice that the back burner was heating up, and my paintbrushes were soaking in a wine glass. Carter hadn't wanted me to sell it, so I'd added an extra zero to the price so it wouldn't attract a buyer. Unfortunately for him, the curators hung it in the entrance as a centerpiece, and one of the first women through the door shrieked, "Omigod, I have to have that!" She bought it on the spot.

I finally grasped the true power of art, exactly what Robert Markle had been trying to teach me all those years ago. Through art, we can be disruptive, make political statements, *say something*, even if it isn't what most people want to hear.

I'D BEEN CONFIDING IN ONE of my oldest friends, Roger Middleton. Roger was a deeply spiritual man and frequently emailed me poems by his favorite poet, Shamsuddin Muhammad, the fourteenth-century Persian lyric poet who used the pseudonym Hafez. When I told Roger that my fears were giving me nightmares, he quoted Hafez: "Fear is the cheapest room in the house. I would like to see you living in better conditions."

Roger and his wife, the Jungian author Sylvia Senensky, were retiring soon, moving out west to Salt Spring Island. As a goodbye gift to the City of Toronto, they'd created a labyrinth in High Park, modeled after the one at Chartres Cathedral outside Paris. "It took us all summer to build it," Roger said, "but it only takes forty minutes to walk it. Why don't you and Jess come for dinner and afterwards we can walk it together!" He claimed that labyrinths have all kinds of healing powers, and it would give me the answers I needed.

I'd learned long ago the difference between a maze and a labyrinth—a maze is meant to trick and confuse, while a labyrinth is meant to soothe and reveal. Dad had once taken us as children to a giant hedge maze in England and taught us the escape trick: "As long as you always keep your right shoulder to the wall, you'll find your way out." This "a-mazed" me and had proven true, even when I put pencil to paper and finished puzzle books in double-quick time. But the strategy hadn't helped at all in my life with Bluebeard; his dangerous emotional mazes seemed impossible to exit, even when I put my shoulder to the wall.

A week later, Jess and I were in Roger and Sylvia's kitchen. "The labyrinth is ancient," Sylvia said. "It goes back to druid times, used by people on a quest." She told us that when we enter a labyrinth and make our way to the center, we are on a journey to remember where we came from— our connection to the earth, the never-ending cycle of birth and death, all that has been and ever will be—to bear witness to the process of creation. Entering a labyrinth takes us back to the beginning. And we exit the same way, in a rebirth. "In our lifetimes," said Sylvia, "we make many journeys to and from the center. It's how we discover the larger story of who we really are and what we can become."

We'd lingered over dinner and the light had faded, but we piled into Roger's car and drove the short distance to High Park. As we pulled into the parking lot near the Grenadier Cafe, the full moon was being chased by heavy clouds. When it disappeared, we were plunged into darkness.

"Through those trees!" said Roger, pointing the way with his flashlight while we stumbled after him. "Just a short walk through the woods to the clearing."

"I still don't understand why you wanted me to bring my sketches," I said, clutching them to my chest.

"You'll see. A labyrinth is holy ground. When you walk it in focus, it becomes a meditative experience. What has been in the dark will move into the light. If you start walking with a question in your mind, you'll have your answer at the end."

"You mean, like how do I let go of all this?"

"Exactly!"

As we neared the clearing, we could hear what sounded like a raucous party—loud sounds of glass smashing on pavement, a clattering of wood, young voices swearing.

"This is unusual," whispered Roger. "Normally, it's all quiet. Wait here while I check." His small beam of light disappeared up a knoll. In a few minutes, he came running back, his light bouncing up and down. "I'm afraid we'll have to turn back. Teenagers are there, smashing things up. I don't like it. It doesn't feel right."

"You sure?" I was disappointed now. In my head, I was already practicing my question: *How to let go? How to let go? How to let go?*

"We can always come back another night," said Sylvia.

"No, let's do it tonight," I said. "Is that okay? I'm not afraid of teenagers."

When we finally broke through the trees, we were at the south end of a large circle of black cement. A labyrinthine path of white paint, glowing eerily in the moonlight, wound its way to the center, reminding me of a cross-section of the brain. The whole circle was surrounded by waist-high wooden bleachers.

Huddled near the entrance, a crowd of people were laughing and shouting. It was impossible to see their features in the dark, but they appeared to be teenage boys. Some were smashing beer bottles against the cement. A few were careening across the labyrinth on skateboards.

Ignoring the commotion, I looked at Roger. "Where do we start?"

"Over there . . ." he whispered, pointing to the west, "at the far end."

Walking slowly, with Roger, Sylvia and Jess in single file behind me, I followed the ghostly path of white paint. Far to the north, I could see the bright golden lights of the city. I clutched my sketches and focused on my question.

We tried to ignore one skateboarder who was buzzing in and out between us, while the shadowy audience on the perimeter began heckling and mocking.

One called out, "Hey! Wha-cha doin' over there?"

Another voice chimed in, "Do your parents know where you are? Ha ha ha."

But suddenly, one loud dissenter shouted, "Leave 'em alone, dickhead!"

Immediately the hecklers hushed, and the skateboarder melted to the sidelines. The dissenter sidled up to me—a tall boy in a black hoodie with his hands jammed into the pockets of his jeans.

"Hey," he said, jerking his chin. "You meditatin' or somethin'?"

"Sort of," I said, my voiced hushed. "We're walking this labyrinth."

"That's what this is?"

"Yep."

"I seen it before but never tried it."

"This is my first time, too," I told him. "The people behind me are the ones who made it."

He looked back at Roger and Sylvia. "No kidding! What's it for?"

"It's like an ancient puzzle. You can walk it to get answers."

"Cool." He hovered beside me indecisively, looking back at his friends.

One of them called out, "Hey! Mo! Suckin' up?"

Lowering his voice, he said to me, "Mind if I walk it with you?"

"By all means. Just follow the lines to the middle and back out again. But it takes a while."

His friend called again, "Hey! Mo!"

"Later, man!"

Once he joined our single file, a respectful silence descended, and I wondered if he was the ringleader. His friends were all watching us. I plodded on.

About twenty minutes later, I arrived at the center and held my sketches high in the air. *How to let go?* At that very instant, the clouds parted, the moon reappeared and I heard the word *forgiveness*. Who said that? I looked into the darkness but saw nothing. From the shadowy perimeter, a few hands began to clap. Then a cheer. I smiled. Was this the answer to my question?

As I turned slowly to begin my journey out, I noticed that Mo was right behind me. Halfway back, the moon retreated. My legs felt heavy, as though I were walking through quicksand. It took all my energy and all my concentration to put one foot in front of the other. What did it mean? I looked at my watch. Another twenty minutes had gone by. How was it possible that such a thin path, painted on such a small patch of cement, could take so long to walk?

As I waited at the finish line for the others to catch up, Mo came over and extended his hand. "Hey man," he said, "thanks for showing me the way!"

"It was my pleasure."

"Name's Mohammad, by the way."

Mohammad? I'd been followed by someone with the name of the poet? Had this labyrinth brought me back full circle—back to Shamsuddin Muhammad and the poems of Hafez? Something was going on, something much bigger than me.

He gave me a high five.

"Hi, Mohammad," I said happily, "my name is Plum."

———

A FEW WEEKS LATER, another email popped into my inbox from Roger:

> *Greet yourself*
> *In your thousand other forms*
> *As you mount the hidden tide and travel*
> *Back home.*
> —HAFEZ

The Psychic

I'M NOT ONE OF those women who looked in the mirror at age twenty-nine and thought, *Yikes, tomorrow I turn thirty!* or rushed to a liquid wake with girlfriends on the eve of my fortieth to cry into my beer. I was always too busy, in love with life. Even my fiftieth passed on a high note: I'd taken a break from Bluebeard—one of my many "final rehearsals"—and friends threw me a party without inviting him. They placed a crown on my head while my children sang bawdy new lyrics they'd written to the tune of "Diamonds on the Soles of Her Shoes." That was the year I made a grand ten-year plan: I'd write a zippy little musical about Alzheimer's called *Cruise of a Lifetime*, staged on a boat, setting my lyrics to tunes borrowed from The Bee Gees. (*Mama Mia* got permission from ABBA, so how hard could it be?) I planned to cast all my friends and rent the Winter Garden Theatre, where on my sixtieth birthday, we'd high-kick and sing our way happily ever after in front of a thousand cheering fans.

Of course, that's not what happened. "Happily ever after" is never the end—remember? The next ten-year chapter was so grueling that *Cruise of a Lifetime* never got written and my sixtieth birthday came and went. By 2009, when I turned sixty-three, I was hanging on by a thread, convinced I had no future at all.

To cheer me up, my children decided to take me to Southern Accent, a restaurant on Markham Street where a psychic sat in the window, someone they could hire for twenty minutes to predict my future in between courses. They didn't invite Mum, though they joked that the restaurant's name evoked the sign in her kitchen: *Y'all Spoken Here!* Mum was a bit of a psychic herself, constantly practicing mental telepathy, trying to get into my head. I'd left her house only a few hours earlier, telling her I had a date.

We parked across from Honest Ed's, already hollowed out and slated for demolition, more or less how I was feeling myself. It seemed like only yesterday when it was our favorite go-to department store where garish neon signs lit up its windows—*Honest Ed's Repulsive!! But His Bargains Are Appealing!*—and when we used to line up with excitement under its screaming banner: *This Way You Lucky People!*

Markham Street was no longer the way I remembered it from my twenties. It was still a touch bohemian with a few artsy stores selling used books and vintage clothing, but like everything else of my generation, it appeared to be falling apart. Suspect Video, the dingy basement shop renting old black-and-white movies, was still open, but most of the other stores were shuttered, their bricks loose, litter drifting in the doorways. It seemed that most of the artists had left. Developers were sniffing around. Mum always said, "You can't stop progress!" But this progress didn't feel like an improvement; it felt like the soul had left the body and vultures were circling the carcass. I sensed a sadness in the air, a forlorn acceptance, as if the fight was over and the world had moved on. The weather didn't help. It was November, cold and gray, with an early dark nearing the end of the year.

Sensing my mood, my kids playfully grabbed my shoulders and wiggled their fingers in my face. "Woo-woo," they chanted, "watch out for voodoo!"

We stumbled up the steps of a crumbling Victorian row house and tickled through beaded curtains into a dimly lit bar where Christmas lights snaked around the perimeter and green tinsel dripped from the ceiling. The warm air was comforting, seasoned with roasted garlic and brown sugar—the spicy aromas of Creole cooking—and the honeyed music of New Orleans jazz spilled from the speakers. We were ushered through to the dining room where Mardi Gras masks grinned from the walls and small wooden booths tented with exotic fabrics lined the walls. Each of my three children had brought their significant other, so seven of us were seated out in the open at a large wooden table.

After bringing us drinks, our waiter arrived with plates full of jambalaya smothered with sassafras, and between the entrée and dessert, the hostess summoned me for my appointment with fate. "Kelly's ready for you now," she said.

My children giggled and clapped. "Yay!" said Virginia. "I can't wait to hear what she tells you."

"What's this for?" said Jess as I took off my rings and handed them to her.

"I don't want to give her any clues."

"Oh, for God's sake. Just don't tell her anything!"

"If you're not back in twenty minutes, we'll call the police!" said Carter, laughing.

The hostess led me around the corner to a hidden alcove beside the front door. She pulled aside a flowered curtain, revealing a tiny room with floor-to-ceiling windowpanes shrouded by leafy-green spider plants. Outside, the darkened street was deserted. Tiny snowflakes had started to fall, swirling and dancing high in the air near a single streetlamp, like moths lured to a light.

Kelly wasn't what I expected. I'd expected something playful, like Honest Ed would have had—a papier-mâché statue in gypsy attire, perhaps, with a slot in her cheek for coins—but instead, I saw a pleasant-looking woman in her late forties with shoulder-length blonde hair, wearing a casual brown sweater and jeans. No turban. No crystal ball.

She was sitting on a bentwood chair with her eyes closed, meditating. A stubby candle flickered on a small wooden table in front of her. I sat down opposite and waited.

Although she said nothing, I felt oddly connected to her, as if a current were passing between us. When her eyes fluttered open, she smiled. Reaching up to a small bookshelf on the wall behind her, she withdrew a pack of tarot cards.

"Please . . ." she said. "Cut these for me."

As I took them from her, I felt an electrical spark and wanted to tell her, in case it was significant, but my skepticism kicked in: *Don't tell her anything!* The cards felt soft and thick, like felted wool, their round edges worn, their surfaces scraped with fine lines. I imagined they were seething with the hopes and fears of others—and why not? After all, we leave behind bits of ourselves on everything we touch—our energy, flakes of skin, even our DNA. Letting my fingertips trickle slowly down the edge of the pack until my inner voice said *STOP*, I lifted a small section and placed it neatly beside.

Kelly probed with small talk as she fiddled with the cards.

"I sense you're an artist," she said. "Perhaps a writer?"

I looked at her, wide-eyed. How could she have known my secret dream? Another psychic had predicted the same thing when I was twenty, but my high school English teacher used to pound on her desk and shout, "Don't write until you have something to say!" which effectively shut me up for the next five decades. What did I have to say that hadn't been said already? Whenever I went into a bookstore and saw discounted books piled high on a remainder table, each one representing years of an author's life, I felt discouraged.

"I see books in your future!" Kelly said.

Then, after running through typical predictions about love, pain and money, she got personal, predicting I'd have a grandson, "born nine months from today." How did she know I even had children? I didn't think she'd seen us enter the restaurant, but maybe she had. Still, it seemed unlikely I'd have a grandchild anytime soon—none of my children were married.

After restacking the deck, Kelly dealt a few cards in a row across the table. I knew nothing about tarot cards, but the first one had crossed swords, which seemed ominous. A warrior was sitting on a chariot pulled by what looked like two sphinxes. In Greek mythology, I knew the sphinx was a monster who devoured anyone who couldn't answer its questions.

"This is a powerful card," said Kelly. "It means you've been tested in the past."

"Gawd—tests!" I said, rolling my eyes. I glanced at her face, but she seemed to be in a serious trance. Why was I interrupting her, trying to make jokes?

"You've had a difficult journey, with still more setbacks ahead." She looked up at me. "But don't lose hope. You can pull through this . . . with more confidence than before."

She flipped over another card. This one showed a hooded, ghostlike figure carrying a lantern. It stirred a distant memory of when I was sixteen and Mum took me to visit the Slade School of Fine Art in England. I shuddered to think what this card might mean.

"The Hermit," said Kelly, reading my thoughts. She tapped the card with her fingernail. "You're about to enter a period of retreat, a time of introspection and insight."

"Does this mean I'll finally understand my mother?"

"Maybe."

When the third card showed a man hanging upside down, dangling from a tree—*uh-oh*—with a rope tied around his leg, Kelly said, "Have you had much upheaval in your life recently?"

"I suppose so," I said, although *upheaval* was not how I'd describe it. *Buried* was more like it. Dad had died a year ago, after a fifteen-year battle with dementia, and now Mum was cranky as hell and on oxygen. Sometimes I thought I'd never claw my way out.

"Then it's time for you to let go."

"But he has a rope tied to his foot!" I said, pointing out the obvious. "How can I let go when I'm all tied up?"

"These images aren't meant to be taken literally." Kelly waved her hand across the table. "They can be interpreted any way you want. It depends whether we're talking about the past, present or future."

"I hope we're not talking about the future!" I laughed. "At my age, I want all my difficult journeys to be *in the past*. Where are all the *happy* cards, showing rainbows and flowers and bluebirds chirping away?" In my head, I was already reinventing the deck, sensing a business opportunity. "Who designed these things?"

But Kelly didn't laugh. After more cards and more inter-pretations, she turned my left hand over to examine my palm. Her long, pointed fingernails were lacquered bright red, studded with tiny diamonds no bigger than pinheads. Tracing my lifeline with her pinky finger as though she were following a map with many forks in the road, suddenly she gasped.

"What?" I said. "What?"

"Show me your other hand."

I extended my right palm across the table for her to compare. Her eyes darted back and forth between them.

"Hon . . ." she said, her eyebrows knitted together, "have you had any near misses . . . any car accidents . . . or any-thing like that?"

"Sure!" I said, still wondering how I could make her laugh. Wasn't this whole exercise meant to be a lighthearted party trick? "I always thought I'd die at forty-two, but that was more than twenty years ago. My brother Chris phoned me on my forty-third birthday and said, 'You still here?' The whole family joked about it."

"So, what happened?"

I tried to remember back to that era. It was the peak of my career. My chaotic life as a single mother was beginning to lighten up. The publishing company I'd founded was doing well, and I'd just fallen crazily in love. It seemed like another lifetime now, drenched in trauma and denial. It was just before Dad's bicycle accident, before his triple bypass. Before Mum went on oxygen. Before Dad began to lose his mind. It was just before Sandy moved back from Saudi Arabia, just before I walked in on him shaving in the bathroom one morning and asked him what that tiny oozing spot was, below his right nipple.

"My brother Sandy died instead."

"Oh," she said, "I'm sorry. But I meant *your* accidents. What happened when you had *your* near misses?"

"I always heard voices." I shrugged. "Warning me."

I told her about the dark night at college in Boston in 1966, when I was walking back to my dorm in the dark after a play rehearsal. My arms were full of books and scripts, and I was about to take the shortcut I always took, a back entrance that led through the garden. As I turned off the sidewalk and up the stone steps, all the nerves in my body suddenly started tingling with a sense of foreboding. A voice in my head screamed, *Look up! Look up!* First, I just saw his eyes . . . the moonlight glinting off his forehead. Then I saw his face. He was hiding behind the stone wall in a tangle of trees and shrubbery, just inside the path . . . waiting for me. My heart started pounding as I raced back down the steps and into the safety of street traffic. I didn't stop running until I'd circled the block and reached the front door of my dorm. I was surprised to find that my heart was pounding again, just at the memory of it.

Then I told her about my premonition in France, shortly after PC and I were married, warning of the snowstorm that almost cost us our lives, and about the day in 1986, when I was zooming along the highway in my little red Honda. A voice in my head screamed, *Watch it—on your right!* I looked in my side mirror, but there was nothing there. The voice kept shouting—louder and more insistent, *Watch it! Watch it!* And, sure enough, within seconds, a little green sports car came roaring up behind me on the inside lane, weaving erratically like a drunk, heading straight for me. I had just enough time to swerve onto the shoulder, out of his way. It left me so shaken I'd had to stop.

But I told her the scariest near miss was when I was crossing a street in 1991, after Sandy died. A taxi accelerated around the corner, looking back over his shoulder as he sped towards me. I didn't hear a voice. I felt arms propelling me high into the air and depositing me onto the opposite curb. It happened so fast that it was like being in an altered reality. At the time, I believed it was my dead brother who had thrown me to safety. I shouted to the strangers passing by, "Did you see that? Did you see that?!" But nobody answered. It was as if the film of my life had been cut and spliced—with the tragedy edited out.

"Is that what you meant?" I said, ticking off the events in my mind, surprised that tiny details from so long ago had come crashing back into memory. I could remember the exact expression on the man's face in the bushes as our eyes locked, the oval decal on the bumper of the green sports car and the canary-yellow suit I was wearing as I fell to the pavement yelling, "Did you see that?!"

"Sounds like you have horseshoes up your yin-yang," Kelly said.

"You think I'm living on borrowed time?"

"I'm just telling you what I see." She pointed to a series of small lines that bisected my lifeline like tiny hairline cracks. "See all these breaks?"

"Lucky breaks?"

"No," she said, "your life should have ended a long time ago."

Exactly. But the only reason Kelly knew this was because I told her so. Why hadn't I kept my mouth shut? I'd never doubted the spirit world, but why would I believe a so-called psychic who came included in a dinner menu?

The spirit world had always felt familiar to me, like an ancient text imprinted on my soul. It's not a belief, it's a knowing—one of those things we're afraid to talk about, one of the last taboos. Who are we? Where did we come from? Where do our souls go after we die? There are just too many stories in our family, too many unexplained coincidences. I refuse to believe that we're nothing but dust.

Throughout my life, I've experienced ESP, automatic writing, spiritual guides and ghosts. I believe in the energy of matter and the connectedness of all things—my children and their father and me; my mother and my father; their parents and their parents' parents—strands that weave and whisper down through the ages in our braided DNA.

I'd recently read that during pregnancy, cells full of DNA can migrate both ways—not just from mothers to babies, as previously detected—but from babies to mothers. Did this mean I'd received some Viking DNA from my ex-husband, via my babies?

If spiritual energy is inherited then that explains some of my own close encounters. I'm hoping my children have received some of this ancient, mysterious energy from me, but whenever I say to my son, "Just trust your *gut!*" he looks at me skeptically, as if he's not sure he has one or how to precisely locate it. I tell him it requires faith in your higher self, in the ability of your spirit to see ahead, around corners, to predict the immediate future. It requires practice, and I've been practicing since childhood.

When I finally made my way back to the table, I felt like I was in a time warp. What had just happened in there?

My children were agog. "What did she say? What did she say?"

Searching for some of the happy trivia Kelly gave me at the start of our session, I winked at them. "She sees a man in my future . . . says his name will start with the letter D."

"Derek? Dennis? Dan?" said Carter, naming some of my previous partners.

"Or Donethat?" said Jess. They were all laughing by then.

"What else?" said Virginia.

"She says I'm a writer. She sees books in my future."

"See? Told you!"

"And supposedly, I'm going to have a *grandson* in nine months' time!"

"A *grandson*?!" They thought this was hilarious. They pointed fingers at each other.

"Ha! It won't be from me."

"Me either."

"Not me—no way!"

"What else did she say?" said Carter. "You were gone much longer than twenty minutes."

"I can't remember," I said, brushing them off. I wanted to wait—to see if any of her other predictions came true. Besides, Mum always told me, "If you could have a crystal ball, you wouldn't want one."

SIX WEEKS AFTER OUR VISIT to the psychic, Virginia pulled me into the kitchen, away from the rest of our family gathered in my dining room for Sunday dinner.

"Guess what?" she whispered. "I'm pregnant!"

"What? You're kidding!"

"Nope—I went to the doctor on Friday!"

"Oh, sweetie, how wonderful. Congratulations!" I gave her a hug. "When's it due?"

"August . . . near Anya's birthday!"

"Omigod, wait till she hears. Her *third* great-grandchild."

"Your *first* grandchild," she reminded me.

"Yes!"

I'd waited overlong for this moment, way past my granny "best before date." It was decades ago when I first got the urge to grandparent. I can still remember when I was in my late forties, standing in the checkout line of a grocery store when a new mother and her pram rolled up behind me. The sight of her baby caused my heart to flood. I *wanted* one of those and I burst into tears. It must have been hormones, the tail end of fertility, the last gasp before menopause, a physiological window of opportunity to rope me back into that unreasonable facsimile of parenthood. In my case, this mood lasted ten years. During that time, I would have been prepared to do anything—babysit all weekend, take on the nighttime feedings, even quit my day job—anything. But without any takers, I diverted my energies elsewhere, and slowly the feelings subsided.

Now, twenty years later, when I could no longer do the splits or carry fifty-pound weights, when I was feeling over-burdened with eldercare and fantasizing about escaping to Fiji, along came this new umbilical cord. It reminded me of one of Frida Kahlo's paintings, her family tree where she looks like she's been disemboweled. What is it about our delayed generations, anyway?

Today's smart young couples seem happy to postpone childbirth. They boast that science has finally enabled them to have children as late as they want. Women can freeze their eggs. Men can freeze their sperm. But what about us? You still can't freeze a grandma.

Or can you?

I suppose we could become cryonauts down in Arizona, paying to have our remains packed with dry ice and immersed in vats of liquid nitrogen, expecting to be thawed out two hundred years from now. They're still checking on Dr. James Bedford, the first grandpa to enter cryonic suspension in 1967. I heard there's a watchman whose job it is to go from vat to vat all night, checking the temperature gauges. But what if he falls asleep? Or the company goes bankrupt? What then?

The next time I visited Virginia, she was giggly with anticipation. Upstairs, she'd transformed her guest room into a baby's room. The shabby chic dresser had a foam pad on top, turning it into a change table. Each drawer held a mass of little girl clothes—frilly pants, smocked dresses and a bubbly turquoise bathing suit the size of my fingernail.

"But you're having a boy," I reminded her, "the psychic said so."

"No," she said with confidence, "it's a girl! I can feel it."

But Kelly was right—the following month, an ultrasound confirmed it was a boy! And, just as she'd predicted, my grandson was born nine months later—*to the day.* How could she have known? Word spread like wildfire, and soon all of Virginia's friends were lining up at Southern Accent to have their tarot cards dished up by Kelly.

On Christmas day, we all drove to Mum's house, where four-month-old Ben was the center of attention. It'd been so long since we'd had a baby in the mix. Through my eyes, he looked exactly like all the other babies in our family: He belonged to our flock. Everyone was saying he looked just like his great-grandmother. He had the same chubby cheeks, the same brown hair tinged with auburn, the same smile that crinkled his nose. He was passed from uncle to aunt and rocked and cuddled, but I was noticing that his great-grandmother paid him almost no attention at all. It was so unlike Mum. Perhaps the chaos was unsettling, the noise too hard on her ears. She sat at the dining room table, hooked up to her oxygen tubing, ignoring his tiny hands reaching out to her from his blanket on the floor by her feet. He smiled and blew bubbles and kicked his chubby legs, but Mum didn't look down. She just stared past him, out the window towards the lake. She picked at her fingernails, as if she was disinterested. That's one of the clues I had missed, evidence that Mum was letting go, already setting her sights on a more distant horizon.

I wasn't prepared. I thought she'd live forever.

MUM DIED THREE WEEKS LATER, in mid-January. She was ninety-three. Well-meaning people say time heals. It doesn't always, but at least the emotional trauma can be reduced to a phrase that rolls off your tongue. I say, "Mum died in 2010," but there's always more to those weighted words. She died after ten years of eldercare, yet when she died, it surprised me. I came blinking into the sunlight like a gopher. What just happened? One minute I'd been a fifty-three-year-old daughter, and suddenly I was a sixty-three-year-old grandmother getting senior discounts at the drugstore. Grief and relief flooded over me in a tangled mess of emotion.

Looking out at Mum's frostbitten garden, at the broken hydrangea stalks bowing their heads to the earth, I knew that by spring, they'd be green again, standing tall, waving their balls of white blossoms towards the sky. I began drawing them in the margins of my notebook as if to reassure myself: love—loss—growth—rebirth. How could it be otherwise? Life is a cycle. Nature teaches us this.

The darkness of February gradually brightened, and the days grew longer. My brothers and I began clearing out Mum's house to get it ready for sale. I moved into her house for what I thought would be a six-week stint. Little did I know that I'd still be there eighteen months later.

By April, most of the closets had been emptied of clothes, the kitchen cupboards emptied of old food and my brothers had finished doing the heavy lifting. All that was left were the documents—but, oh, the documents! The most precious inheritance of all.

I marveled at what Mum had saved—the theater stubs, dry cleaning receipts, postcards from Trout Run, Pennsylvania . . . our whole family history was there. Every breadcrumb triggered memories for me, and every night I wrote them down. I thought I was saying goodbye to the past, but the cascade of stories catapulted me forward, into a new beginning.

One afternoon, as I sat cross-legged on the floor of Mum's living room sorting through a pile of old papers, I emptied a bulging manilla envelope and realized the contents were mine. Unknown to me, Mum had been saving my literary efforts: illustrated stories written when I was five, poems and essays from high school and a newspaper clipping describing a play I'd produced at the local library when I was eleven. I looked in disbelief at the stash. What had happened to my dreams? It was as if Mum had left me a forgotten map to the interior of my soul, as if she wanted to *remind* me.

And then a letter emerged—a rejection letter sent to me by a publisher in 1972. As I scanned the first line, "We are returning your manuscript . . . ," a flood of emotion hit me. I remembered the crushing blow all those years ago, the finality of those words, how they confirmed my belief that my work was worth nothing. I didn't remember the rest of the letter, but I did remember running to Mum in tears. Why I ran to her, when I was married by then with children of my own, I have no idea, but she'd saved that letter and here it was, crumpled and tear stained.

Pouring myself a glass of wine, I smoothed out the letter and sat down at the kitchen table to reread the whole thing, to face the bitter truth of criticism: "We are returning your manuscript . . . for one reason only. We already have three similar books in our line. But your efforts are tremendous, and I encourage you to do more and submit them to us."

Wait a minute . . . I took this as *rejection*? I couldn't believe what I was reading. Had I buckled under so light a breeze? The publisher continued: ". . . your talent is a real treat to see." He even attaches glowing comments from his senior editor, who added: "I hope she writes to us again."

I couldn't decide whether to shoot myself or track down the publisher. I wondered if he was still alive. After a few more drinks, I googled him and found him—on Facebook—long-since retired. As a joke, I messaged him with a scan of his old letter and told him I was ready now. Just following up. He replied that he was very pleased to hear from me, even though *forty years* had gone by!

What had happened to me in those intervening years? I thought of all the things I'd tried to write, all my false starts: the poems for Pierre, old half-written novels, the stories for my children, even *The Mouse and the Hat* that I'd written when I was five years old. What was I afraid of—success or failure?

Later that night, I opened Dad's old credenza and placed his favorite LP on the turntable. Vera Lynn was singing Rose of England, the famous World War II song, full of love and longing. I lay back on Mum's chintz-covered sofa and closed my eyes, trying to close the gap of seventy years, to picture Mum and Dad back in London, falling in love as the bombs were dropping. As the record neared its end, the needle hit a snag: Vera kept repeating *thou shalt , , , thou shalt . . . thou shalt . . .*

Irritated, I gave the credenza a little kick, and Vera completed her song: *Thou shalt blossom to the end of time!*

Is that all it takes—a little kick?

The End Is My Beginning

THE FOLLOWING WEEK, I made a run to the thrift store, hauling the last of Mum's things that none of us wanted, and what I saw there alarmed me—piles and piles of identical stuff from our parents' generation, as if they were dying *en masse*. And, of course, they were! After all, we were the baby boomers. At each stage of life, our sheer numbers created a bubble, like a coagulation of plaque moving through an artery. Obviously, we were all clearing out our parents' homes at the exact same moment in history. My first thought was *It looks like we're throwing away the whole of the twentieth century!* My next thought was *Why is no one writing about this?*

Perhaps the psychic's prediction one year earlier had planted the seed. Perhaps she'd given me confidence to see myself as a writer. There was no question that her predictions were starting to come true. After all, my grandson had been born nine months to the day, so maybe there really were books in my future.

I could feel the spirits hovering.

The next morning, walking through the local library, I saw a sign for a six-week memoir class and thought, *This must be fate*. I ran to sign up.

"I'm sorry," said the librarian. "That class is full."

"You don't understand," I said, now deciding to ignore fate, "I have a book to write!" I thought of all the memories I'd recorded in my notebooks over the past nine months.

"Perhaps you'd like to come back next year?"

Next year? Was she crazy? I'd already wasted forty years.

In the library, they had so many titles on how to write a memoir, they had a section all their own, and I couldn't help wondering if every baby boomer, now faced with their own mortality, suddenly felt the urge to write one. Perhaps we wanted to be remembered by something other than a chenille bedspread. Is this what my cousin had meant when she said to me after Mum's funeral, "How does it feel, now that you have your back to the wall?" I checked out as many how-to books as I could carry, and William Zinsser's *On Writing Well* became my bible.

But what did I want to say?

In a rush of inspiration, I wrote a book proposal for *They Left Us Everything*. I knew it had to be catchy enough to interest a publisher, so I described it as a "*Goodnight Moon* for adults." That's how I was feeling: like a clingy, grieving adult child needing to say goodnight to every, single, thing. Margaret Wise Brown's "goodnights" kept coming into my mind as I emptied Mum's house: *Goodnight, chairs . . . Goodnight, clocks . . .*

Over the next nine months, the book poured out, almost fully formed, as if the stories had been accumulating in my brain since childhood. Mum's house hadn't sold, so I was still living there on the lake, watching the sky, listening to the geese, reconnecting with the landscape of my childhood. The landscape appeared so serene and beautiful . . . but a minefield can look like that. I'd spent my life sidestepping danger zones; perhaps it was time to deactivate them in a controlled explosion before I got blown up. It seemed I'd abandoned my children in Toronto, needing instead to repair my relationship with Mum. We had a much better relationship now that she had died because I finally let her into my life. The veil between this world and infinity—the ongoing river of time—felt almost transparent. I was speaking to Mum all the time. It turns out that she'd been hiding in the draft all along, waiting to be uncovered.

"This isn't a book about clearing out a house," the editor said. "It's about your relationship with your mother! You need to go deeper."

Going deeper was terrifying. How could I write about that? The murder of crows that usually perched on my shoulder flew back and forth, cackling, *Your work sucks! Caw! Caw! Let's eat her for breakfast!* I worried I'd been an ungrateful daughter, that I wouldn't do Mum justice, that I was the only daughter on earth who'd ever had such a torturous end-of-life relationship with her mother, that I might be arrested for some of the thoughts that had gone through my head. What would people think?

But once the book was published, at my very first public appearance, a reader gave me a hug and whispered in my ear, "I had a mother just like yours."

It turns out there were a lot of us.

ORIGINALLY, I'D PLANNED TO complete my manuscript in Paris—isn't that what all authors do? I had this romantic vision of sitting in an outdoor café—preferably smoking, sipping espresso and wearing a beret—penning a prologue that I could sign with cachet: *Plum Johnson, Paris*. I'd even swapped my house in Toronto for an apartment near the Bois de Boulogne for the month of October. The trouble was there was no prologue; I'd finished the book in September.

I still didn't know what my book was about. When the publicists at Penguin tried to rehearse me for press interviews, I'd said, "It's about cleaning out Mum's house," and they laughed. "You can't say that! Nobody wants to read a book about cleaning out a house." They tried to give me new language: "It's about *inheritance* . . . about *house as container* . . . about *your relationship with your mother!*" But I was still thinking, sadly, *Goodnight chairs* . . . *Goodnight clocks* . . . *Goodnight house by the lake* . . .

The Paris apartment was grand, but I felt emptied, with nothing to do but wait. Tiny wrought iron balconies at each tall French window were filled with pots of red geraniums. Each morning, I watched as sleepy occupants in the apartment opposite heaved their duvets over the railings to air. Outside the kitchen window, two pigeons ruffled their feathers on the ledge as the laughter of children filtered up from the school courtyard below.

During the day, I leafed through books at Shakespeare and Company, sketched in the Tuileries Garden and searched out hidden art galleries. At Galerie Maeght, I splurged on a book of silkscreened fairy tales by Warja Lavater, with pages of richly colored graphic symbols that reminded me of my childhood Parcheesi board. Her books have no words, which is how fairy tales ought to be told.

At first, I felt lonely. Each time I stopped at a café for espresso, I wished Mum were with me. Strolling along the Seine, I missed Lake Ontario and wished I'd swapped my house for an apartment in Oakville, instead. And then, one afternoon, after poking around some fabric shops near Montmartre, I got to the top of Rue Seveste, turned a corner onto Rue Ronsard and stumbled upon an unexpected treasure: the Musée d'Art Naif in Halle Saint-Pierre.

Here, in the ancient brick pavilion with its soaring arched windows, was an exhibit of l'art brut where strange, warped, outsider art filled the walls. Here, women like Aurélie Levaux and Isabelle Pralong had embroidered complex, gut-wrenching narratives on silk. Here, my sampler child had sisters! My breastplates and finger bowls had cousins!

Halfway around the world, I'd found my tribe.

THE FIRST THING I DID when I returned home was run to the phone and listen to an old message I'd saved of Mum's. Listening to her voice now made me happy.

"Happy birthday, m'darling!" she said, in perpetuity. "I'll call later."

Mum's house finally sold, just as my memoir was going to press. The new owners gutted it, raised it off its haunches and scraped it to the bone. From time to time, I drove by to watch as it underwent an editing process of its own. Old passages were removed and new spaces added. My heart fluttered as I watched, as if a close family member were having a massive, lifesaving operation: brain surgery, liver transplant, a quadruple bypass. I felt worried, but hopeful.

Mum's voice echoed: *Nothing lasts forever . . . you can't stop progress!*

I hoped it was progress. The house and I were both beginning new chapters.

I'D OVERHEARD A PUBLISHER referring to my memoir as a "small book," meaning they didn't expect it to sell many copies, but that winter, we learned that *They Left Us Everything* had been nominated for the RBC Taylor Prize, one of the most prestigious awards for literary nonfiction in Canada. My children were ecstatic, but I felt like an imposter. There must have been some mistake. Where was my MFA in creative writing? I'd never studied in Iowa or been invited to Yaddo. I hadn't even spent my twenties interning for a woman's magazine in New York City. What if someone asked me what my credentials were? How on earth did I get on the list?

Brimming with insecurities, I rushed to sign up for an online course in creative writing with Allyson Latta at the University of Toronto and spent the snowy months glued to my computer, completing assignments. Meeting a new group of supportive fellow writers calmed me down; I wasn't alone with my insecurities. We were all facing down the blank page . . . and finally, I had some credentials!

In the spring, I was still on the prize list, shortened now to five finalists. As the festivities kicked into high gear, we were all given interviews with the press. My first interview was with a TV station, and I was petrified by the question I assumed they would pose: *Tell us what your book is about.*

"What if they ask me that?" I whined to my agent for the umpteenth time.

"Why don't you have a chat with Catherine Gildiner?" she said. "She'll give you good advice."

I'd never met Cathy, although I'd been a fan of her memoirs ever since Mum gave me *Too Close to the Falls*. She's

a wonderful writer, but more importantly, she was a psycho-
therapist. My agent offered to make the introduction.

"I understand you have a problem," said Cathy when I
finally got up the nerve to call her.

"Yes," I sniveled into the phone. "I'm terrified that someone will ask me what my book is about, and I won't know
what to say!"

"Don't be ridiculous," said Cathy. "Of course, you know
what your book is about. You wrote it."

"But what if I freeze?"

"Look," she said briskly, "all you need is really good
makeup!"

Then, in the kind of slow, authoritative voice that I
imagined she used with trauma patients, she said, "Here's
what I want you to do. Got a pen? Write this down. Tomorrow morning, I want you to go to this boutique, buy the
most expensive makeup you can find, slather it all over
your face and walk across the street to the TV studio. You'll
be just fine."

The next morning, I did exactly what she told me: I
bought the most expensive makeup I could find, slathered
it all over my face and walked across the street to the TV
studio feeling like I had a layer of cling wrap stretched across
my cheeks. The anchors on the morning show were brimming with enthusiasm, perky in their little sheath dresses and
stilettoes; perfectly groomed, not a hair out of place. I worried that my teeth were too crooked, not white enough; that
my neck sagged like a turkey. In what felt like thirty seconds,

the twenty-minute interview was over. But Cathy was right—
not a single person asked me what my book was about!

PRIZE DAY WAS HELD IN the ballroom of the King Edward
Hotel. Normally, I traveled by subway, but I'd splurged and
taken a taxi. By late morning, the lobby was packed with
editors, publishers, agents and publicists, all milling about,
pecking each other on the cheek. I craned my neck, hoping
to see a familiar face, searching the crowd for Virginia, waiting for my agent to arrive. She had called me the night before,
suggesting I prepare an acceptance speech. "You might have
a chance," she said.

I'd laughed. "Sam, if there's one thing I *don't* have to do
tonight, it's write an acceptance speech! I'm not even going
to wash my hair."

Besides, I already knew who should win and I'd been
practicing my fist pump so I could jump up in the air and
shout yay! when their name was announced.

The ballroom was high-ceilinged and sparkling, filled
with tables clothed in white, laid with crystal and silverware.
Giant posters of the shortlisted authors and their books
hung around the walls. A stage lined one wall, with a podium
and chairs for the jury. Virginia and I found our seats. We'd
been assigned a table in the furthest corner of the room. My
agent, publicist and publisher were seated with us.

After a lavish meal with wine and dessert, each author
was called to the stage and presented with a leather-bound

copy of their book. I was called up last. Smoothing my hand over the cover, feeling the title on the spine—*They Left Us Everything*, embossed in gold—I thought it was the most beautiful thing I'd ever seen. My nose started to run—it always does when I'm nervous—so I grabbed the hanky out of my back pocket. I descended the steps from the stage and made my way back to my table, but just as I sat down, I heard Noreen Taylor, founder of the prize, squeal, "Oh, Plum!" In the distance, I could see she was waving something white in the air. Thinking I'd dropped my dirty hanky and she was holding it up to ask if it was mine, I was momentarily embarrassed, then confused. The place erupted with applause. Virginia reached over to hug me.

It had been eleven years since a female author had won, and when I registered what was happening, I went into shock. I stumbled back up to the podium, where Noreen was waving the white envelope. I have no memory of what I said, but I remember thinking that Mum had orchestrated this—helping me finally achieve what I'd wanted to do since childhood, when I sat on her bedroom carpet and foresaw a published book of mine on her bedside table.

AS A CHILD, THE TRAVELING MUSICIANS was one of my favorite fairy tales. It's the story of four aging animals—a donkey, dog, cat and rooster—whose owners decide they're no longer useful. Mistreated, kicked out and left to die, they meet up in the woods and realize they each have a unique sound; if they band together, they can reinvent their purpose. "Something better than death we can find anywhere!" they shout to each other, and off they go to Bremen to become musicians.

Along the way, they come across a house in the woods with a very high window. In order to see what's inside, they have to stand on each other's shoulders, forming a totem that's more powerful together than alone. What they find are robbers, counting their ill-gotten gain, but the old animals use their unique voices to scare the robbers away and win the day!

The message I got was that you're never too old to create an exciting adventure with like-minded friends; together, your voices have power.

The older I get, the more I see that I often stood on the shoulders of older female friends who lifted me up. They could share their wisdom of what they'd learned on the ground, while I could tell them what I saw ahead through the window. Women often move through life like this, mentoring and being mentored. The female role models in my life exemplified the spirit of reinvention. Even though their lives were interrupted many times over by domestic obligations, they never stopped exploring their artistic selves. I saw that the reinvention of self is what keeps us young and vital. Curiosity unleashes our creativity and takes us to the artist within, that unconstrained space inside our head, the infinite possibilities of our imagination. You never know where life can take you. I treasured those friends whose time was almost up, and now they're gone. I'm taking their place—but not for long; the final culling of our generation is underway. I'm one of the old animals now, wanting those on my shoulders to tell me what they can see up ahead.

In 2017, Pat still lived alone at the age of ninety-eight, pushing ahead on her walker, steely and focused, determined to keep living her best life. I asked her once what her secret was. "Dear," she said, "aging is a slippery slope, and the secret is to *never recline*. Just stay *upright* and grab as many branches as you can on the way down!"

On a warm Sunday morning in late spring, I picked her up and we drove to a bustling family-run Italian bakery on St. Clair Avenue West. The sidewalk was filled with young families: children on scooters, babies in strollers and older couples returning from church, all greeting each other as the streetcars rumbled by. I wanted her help interpreting my dreams; I'd been having so many lately. I knew that Pat had been a member of the Jungian Society since its earliest founding in Toronto. She'd also spent years analyzing her own dreams with Helen Luke at Apple Farm Community, the Jungian retreat center in Three Rivers, Michigan.

We took our café lattes outside to one of the tiny metal tables that were chained to the tree trunks, and Pat slung her handbag over the bars of her walker, turning her face to the sun. We spoke about our marriages and children. As a fashion model in England, Pat had met a much older artist when she was only eighteen; she married him and produced four children. Two of her children had died: her firstborn, a toddler daughter; and many years later, her son, killed by a car shortly after her husband died. So many sorrows had given her enormous spiritual wisdom and strength.

"Why did I waste so many years chasing fairy tales?" I asked. "What was it all for? Was it fate?"

Pat looked at me quizzically: "'The fault, dear Brutus, is not in our stars, but in ourselves.'"

"How on earth do you remember that line?" I was astonished. Pat was almost one hundred years old. I couldn't even remember what somebody told me yesterday.

"Because I was in that play once."

"You were? In *Julius Caesar*?" I was trying to picture Pat as Cassius.

"No, no . . ." Pat laughed. "*Dear Brutus*, by J.M. Barrie! I played the child when I was thirteen, 1932 or thereabouts. It was a repertory company in a small theater in London. In Baker Street, I think. My last line was 'Daddy, come back! I don't want to be a might-have-been.'"

"Ha! That's probably everyone's last line," I said. "I always wonder what I might have been, don't you? What if I'd been born in a different era . . . to a different family . . . in a different country? What if I'd married a different man . . . or studied at a different school?"

Pat took a sip of her latte and looked me in the eye. "You're not a might-have-been."

"What am I then . . . a has-been?"

"No! You're much stronger than you think. After every failed relationship, you've reinvented yourself."

"Yes, but all that reinvention is coming back to haunt me. When I look back on my life, there's no continuity, no *pattern* to my life."

"Reinvention *is* your pattern! It's *everyone's* pattern. It's difficult to see when you're ending one cycle and your new one hasn't yet begun. You need patience. It takes time."

"But time is running out! I feel like I'm at a dead end."

"There's never a dead end, dear, only change. The older I get, the more I believe it. This business of synchronicity, of guidance . . . we don't recognize it when we're younger. For instance, my stone carving. The last piece of stone I got was like hell. I couldn't even get into it! It was worse than granite, quite impossible to carve. And I knew it was a sign."

"A sign of what?"

"Can't you see? Time to stop!"

"Stop and do what?"

"Stop and *wait.* I'm talking about the creative experience. I'm talking about a sign that says 'This is where you're at— don't resist.' It's about the need to lie fallow and the faith required to know that this is what it is, and not some failure. No field produces good crops year after year. You need rest and change. It's about letting go. You're in a different space when you let go."

"But I've been having so many more dreams these days. My subconscious working overtime, I guess."

"Dreams are marvelous things."

"Yes, but recently Bluebeard's been reappearing in mine. In one, he's surrounded by all these women, and he hands me a key."

"That sounds significant."

"Actually, once I woke up, I couldn't remember who handed me the key, maybe one of the women."

"Maybe it doesn't matter. The point is it was *the key*."

"There was more. After I got the key, I tried to go home. It was very late. I had a long drive ahead. We were at a conference in a big hotel in Toronto, and 'home' was my childhood home, in Oakville. I started to descend these stairs to the parking garage. But the stairs were made of marble, narrow and tightly winding, with smooth high walls, like the kind you find in a castle turret. I heard moaning coming from the bottom, but I couldn't see around the corners, and I felt very afraid. The lower I went, the louder the moans. Someone had clearly been in danger and now was in a lot of pain. I decided not to go down any further . . . and that's when I woke up."

"The shape of the stairs is very interesting," said Pat, "full of twists and turns. Narrow and constricting, with no ability to see ahead. And a tower structure—maybe a self-imposed prison? You need to get to the bottom of it, to get 'home.' But you're afraid, so you decided not to go further . . . but maybe you need to. Maybe you're the one who's moaning at the bottom. Maybe it's your own pain you need to confront."

"But the next night, I had another dream where Bluebeard takes me by the shoulders, looks sincerely into my eyes, and says, 'I was only trying to do my best, I was only trying to do my best!'"

"How did you feel when he said that?"

"Like he was asking for forgiveness, I guess. He knew his best wasn't good enough."

"Could that be *the key*? Forgiving him is letting go?"

"That's what I heard in the labyrinth, too, but it hasn't worked."

"Maybe the person you need to forgive is *yourself*!"

SINCE I BEGAN WRITING THIS BOOK, the old Honest Ed's building has been demolished, along with most of the other Victorian buildings on that block, replaced by a massive steel-and-glass housing development that's still under construction. Southern Accent has found a new location, and the psychic has moved away. Books change even as you write them, and that has been true for this one. It hasn't turned out as I thought. I was searching for something when I began, the answer to the question *Who am I?* and perhaps this is impossible to know. I've concluded I really was unconscious in my youth, asleep at the switch as I feared, as unconscious as any of the heroines in fairy tales, even when I thought I'd been "kissed awake."

I still like my title—*The Trouble with Fairy Tales*—hoping to show how a woman's life is constantly interrupted by the lure of lust, the vagaries of fate, the unalterable inheritance of biology. But yesterday I printed out 220 pages and spread them out on my living room floor and decided it was all too contrived. With all the disasters going on in the world, is my story even relevant anymore? Was my life only a series of blood-curdling fairy tales from the Brothers Grimm? Isn't there more to my life story than that? Besides, my daughter Virginia just emailed me an article describing how fairy tales are the "in thing" this year. All kinds of authors are writing about them. She meant it as encouragement, but it's taken the wind out of my sails. I hate being part of a trend. Perhaps I need a new title, something more uplifting, like *The End Is My Beginning*. That's more how I feel. But for this, I would need a new structure.

In my notebook, I draw a circle. It's more in keeping with this new theme. My story can begin and end at the same place. But even this structure seems too simplistic somehow. Traditionally, men lived a linear life, the heroic provider, straight as an arrow from here to there—they were fed fairy tales, too—but how to describe a woman's life, with all the interruptions that loop in and out, causing us to veer off course?

Is it a spiral?

After doodling all day, I finally draw the sign for infinity. It offers a flexible path for adding flashbacks and shifting tenses. I can start the story anywhere. But where? Should I start in the middle, where the loops twist and overlap? Or should I begin somewhere at a point on the side?

I start cutting my manuscript into strips, shifting scenes around. It starts well, but within two days, I have so many different bits and pieces, I can no longer remember where I am. Panic sets in. I feel like Hansel and Gretel, unable to follow the breadcrumbs back home. Perhaps my first title was the right one. Perhaps my life was only a bunch of fairy tales after all. Maybe I'm not a writer. Who am I? How can I not know, after more than seventy years?

Jess phones, and I tell her of my panic.

"My manuscript is a mess!" I cry. "After all this work, I still haven't answered the question I asked at the beginning of the book!"

"What question is that?"

"The main question! WHO AM I?"

"That's the age-old question we can never answer," she says calmly, "because we're always changing. Once you can answer that, there's no point in living."

An hour later, she calls me back, worried she's been too critical. "Why don't we book an appointment with Kelly?" she says. "Just for fun."

"I don't need a *psychic*," I say, exasperated. "I need a *psychiatrist*."

"But psychics make you feel better!"

It takes some time to track Kelly down, but when we do, it turns out she lives near the lake. Her narrow clapboard house seems as tiny as the alcove where she once worked inside the restaurant, and it has the same eclectic vibe. The sofa is a repurposed box spring covered with a patchwork quilt, and an overturned orange crate serves as a table. All the curtains are drawn, candles are lit and an ancient arthritic dog lies curled in one corner. Even in the middle of a sunny afternoon, it feels dark and mysterious, where dreams are made.

"Have I seen you before?" says Kelly.

She doesn't remember me from eight years ago. Her hair is pulled into a ponytail now and blonder than it used to be. Gone are her red lacquered nails. She asks me to stand while she prepares a smudge stick, and when she strikes a match and lights it, the huge bunch of dried weeds and herbs crackles and flares so high, I'm afraid the curtains will catch fire and consume the whole house. Immediately, the room fills with choking smoke. The old dog staggers to his feet, limps around in a circle and slumps back down. Kelly wafts the branches around my body, claiming to see an emerging lioness.

"The lioness symbolizes creativity and power," she says, "intuitive power—motherhood and strength." Immediately, I feel flattered. *Yes*, I think, *a lioness—that's me!* I've left Jessica outside on the porch and now I wish she could hear this.

Suddenly, Kelly begins frantically waving the smoke out of the way and says, "Oh! Is there a grandmother . . . or a mother . . . named *Anne*?"

Mum is the lioness? How could Kelly possibly know her name? I never mentioned it, even eight years ago.

"Yes," I mumble, overcome with awe, "both."

"Good," says Kelly. "Because she's right here . . . hovering all around you."

Of course she is.

She's been hovering ever since she died, her atoms still circulating, proving to me that the dead have more power than the living. Think of the power we bestow on the dead! On the way to their funerals, we stop traffic for them; we call them angels, put them on pedestals, offer up prayers and even hold seances to try and bring them back down to earth. Sometimes they arrive as birds, perched on the windowsills of our peripheral vision. They inhabit our brains. After Mum died, I spoke to her all the time. By the time I'd published my memoir about her, she'd been dead for four years, yet still she accompanied me to the awards ceremony. I stood there on the podium, marveling at how the jury had succumbed to her psychic powers, letting her pick the winner.

PAT GOSS DIED IN 2020 at the age of 101. She was finally persuaded to move out of her house and into a retirement home for the last two years of her life. She didn't want to move, but she did it for the sake of those who loved her, who constantly worried about her safety. Sadly, her final months coincided with the Covid pandemic, so I wasn't permitted to visit. From time to time, I dropped off her favorite pastries at the entrance, feeling powerless and sad. By then, she'd been moved to a palliative care floor, unable to receive phone calls. Our conversations continued, if only in my head.

I've never believed death is the end. I believe it's simply the end of one journey and the start of another. You don't have to believe it if you don't want to, but it's more comforting if you do. There's no proof either way—unless you've encountered a ghost, like I have, or have an open mind to research like that of the late neuropsychiatrist Peter Fenwick who in 1995 wrote *The Truth in the Light: An Investigation of Over 300 Near-Death Experiences.*

A few years back, when my grandchildren came for supper, I slipped this idea nimbly into our conversation. Some people might think it's totally unethical for me to foist my spiritual beliefs onto my innocent offspring, but someone like Elon Musk is going to compete for most of their available brain space anyway, so I consider it an investment in my future. Besides, I want to have someone to talk to after I'm gone.

Four-year-old Georgia was across from me, sitting on the thick dictionary I'd repurposed as a booster seat, and six-year-old Ben was sitting on the flat atlas, his mouth full of spaghetti and carrots.

"My mummy was in your tummy!" Georgia said suddenly in revelation, her spoon raised in midair.

"That's right."

"I was in my mummy's tummy, too," she whispered, as if this bound us in a female conspiracy. In the very next breath, she said, "Will you die?"

"Yes," I said. "Eventually."

"When?"

"Sometime in the next twenty years."

She tilted her head shyly and smiled. "Will you miss Mummy?"

"No, I won't miss anybody because I'll be dead. But your mummy will miss me. You will, too, I hope. But you'll be able to talk to me anytime you want."

"For real?" said Ben, wide-eyed.

"Sure! I'll be listening. I'll answer you."

"How do you know?" said Georgia.

"Because I speak to my mummy all the time, and she's dead."

"Does she answer?"

"Yep."

LONG AGO, AFTER THE BREAKUP of my marriage in 1980, when I was carpooling a gaggle of neighborhood children to school one day, I overheard them in the back seat discussing breakup tapes. According to them, every divorced parent had one—a song they played, over and over, until their kids were sick of hearing it.

"What's *your* dad's breakup tape?" I heard one ten-year-old ask.

"Neil Diamond," said my daughter, "'Love on the Rocks.'"

"What about your mom?"

"Marianne Faithfull," said my son, "'The Ballad of Lucy Jordan.'"

It's stunning what children observe and the language they devise to describe it. I didn't even know that breakup tapes were a thing.

Recently, my adult children reminded me of this. We were standing around the kitchen reminiscing about the "old days," when we first moved into this house.

"We used to hear you dancing to 'Lucy Jordan' every night," Carter said.

"I know," I said, smiling at the happy memory. "The tape deck was in the front hall back then, remember? I used to crank it up so loud."

"But, Mom, that song was about suicide!"

"It was?"

"Didn't you *know*?"

"No! I thought it was about *freedom*—about driving through Paris with the wind in my hair!"

"That part about the wind?" he said, rolling his eyes. "It's where she jumps."

"What?!" I was mortified. How could such a metaphor have flown over my head, especially when the feeling of freedom had lasted for decades! Why didn't I listen more carefully to lyrics?

About a month later, they told me to pack. "Nothing fancy," they said cryptically, "just a quick weekend holiday."

I'd expected a road trip, but late Friday afternoon, they brandished my passport and drove me to the airport, where we boarded an overnight flight. Eight hours later, we were *dans un taxi* careening through Paris with the windows wide open. We screeched to a halt near the top of Montmartre at a tiny hotel with no elevator, just miles and miles of lacy railings leading up a narrow spiral staircase to a room in the attic with two double beds.

For three unforgettable days, we strolled by the Seine, tripped through the Louvre, shopped Au Printemps and ate on the streets, sharing croque-monsieurs by the Eiffel Tower. We never stopped laughing . . . and flew home on Monday. Naturally, my children used up all their airline points—*mais oui!*—but it was much more imaginative than driving me to Niagara Falls. That story, and many others from the spiral trajectory of my life, was missing from *The Blue Fairy Book*. Obviously, the Brothers Grimm never wandered the woods with children like mine.

It wasn't the life I expected, but it does have a happy ending . . . and I did drive through Paris with the wind in my hair!

Afterword

AT THE BEGINNING OF THIS BOOK, I wrote: "The trouble with fairy tales is that they're *not true*," but after recalling my Bluebeard experience, I've had second thoughts: Perhaps the trouble with fairy tales is that they *are* true; perhaps they've *always* been true—stories disguised as fiction hundreds or thousands of years ago by women whose true stories were never believed; silenced, then as now. We should take them as warnings, yes, but they are also mirrors. In her memoir, *Plant Dreaming Deep*, May Sarton wrote: "We have to make myths of our lives; it is the only way to live them without despair."

Acknowledgments

I've been churning over the ideas in this manuscript since 2018—first with my beloved agent and always-first-reader, Samantha Haywood, and then with close friends. Thank you to each and every one who wandered with me through leafy ravines or strolled along the lakeshore or curled up over coffee in living rooms and kitchens, mulling the meaning of fairy tales and the daemon lover; endless, angst-ridden miles of discussions for seven years, more time than I spent on many of my romantic relationships. I'm grateful to Tracy Bordian for her early editorial advice, and to Penguin Canada for their belief in this project. Thank you to the editorial team of Marion Garner, Nicole Winstanley,

Lara Hinchberger, Chloe Gandy, Diane Turbide and Aruna Dahanayake; the production team of Kate Sinclair, Catherine Dorton, Alanna McMullen and Brittany Larkin; and the marketing team of Catherine Knowles, Beth Cockeram and Natasha Tsakiris. And thank you, as always, to my children, who encouraged me through many rough drafts.

PLUM JOHNSON is an author and artist living in Toronto. Her 2014 memoir, *They Left Us Everything*, won the RBC Taylor Prize and was a #1 national bestseller.